FLORENCE

Already published in this series

ALGERIA

AUSTRIA

CÔTE D'AZUR

GARDENS OF ROME

GREECE

ITALIAN LAKES

LONDON

MONT BLANC AND THE SEVEN VALLEYS

NAPLES

PARIS

ROME

SIENNA

SPAIN

VENICE

VERSAILLES

YUGOSLAVIA

In preparation

PROVENCE (new edition)

CHÂTEAUX OF THE LOIRE

Y. AND E.-R. LABANDE

FLORENCE

Translated by JANE HOWITT

with 180 heliogravure illustrations

COVER PAINTING BY YVES BRAYER

NEW YORK
OXFORD UNIVERSITY PRESS
1962

First published in French by
B. ARTHAUD (PARIS AND GRENOBLE)

English text of revised edition © 1962 Nicholas Kaye Limited

PRINTED IN FRANCE

CONTENTS

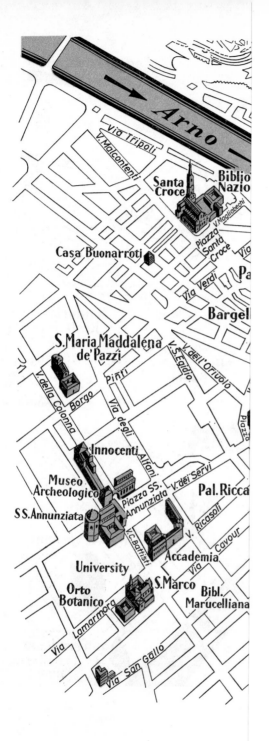
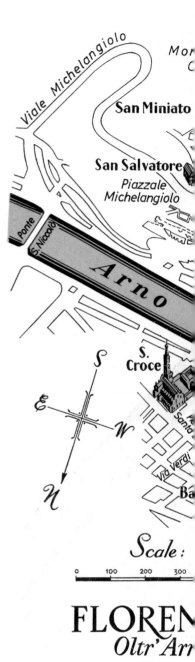

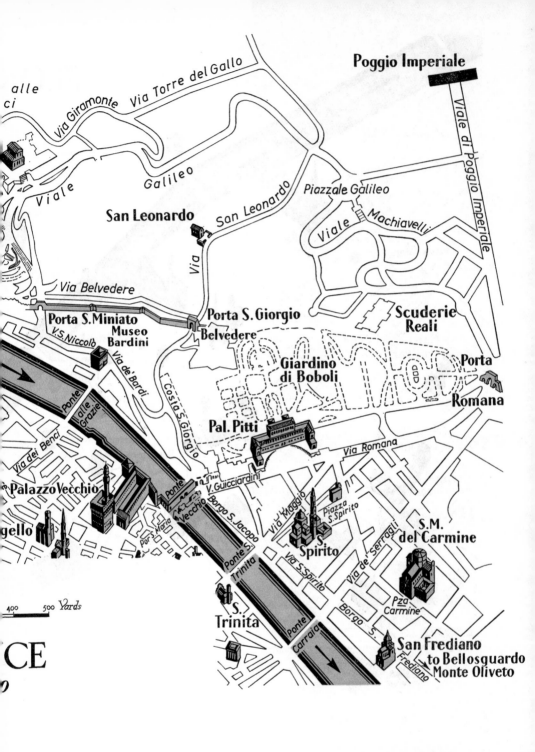

LIST OF ILLUSTRATIONS

GENERAL

MONUMENTS, MUSEUMS AND GALLERIES

OUTSIDE THE CITY

NEAR FLORENCE

FOREWORD

On an impetuous river in the heart of the Italian peninsula there stands a city whose past seems to imitate that river in its violence and contrasts. Apart from Rome, no other Italian city is so renowned in western Europe except Venice which can claim parity but no more. But how well is Florence really known, for all its fame?

This unassuming book was written for those who know the city only by name and repute and seek a closer understanding, and, too, for those who have visited it briefly, maybe, and wish to relive the short time of their stay. It is not a guide, in the proper sense, though in part it follows the same plan and system. The reader will understand that its scope is limited by its size.

The artistic riches of the city of the Red Lily — the flower whose arrogant beauty is linked with the pride in the faces modelled by Mino da Fiesole — are innumerable. Some are unavoidable in their magnificence. For others we must find our way through streets where palace-fortresses loom on either side, or along the lungarni with their celebrated vistas, and go in search of the real Florence.

In order to bring out the city's essential qualities the tour is prefaced with a brief survey of Tuscany and its history, and a glance at the character of its people. To give a clearer picture of the town, our exploration will begin at Fiesole, the home of the first inhabitants, and conclude on those pleasant heights where, in the years of their splendour, the Florentines built the most sedate villas — but not the least pleasant — in Italy. For Florentine culture can only be understood in relation to both the city and the province.

It is the authors' hope that through these pages Florence may become better known and understood, and therefore better loved — as this queen of cities deserves.

Y. and E.-R. L.

VIEW OF FLORENCE FROM SAN MINIATO

THE CITY AND THE HILLS TOWARDS FIESOLE

INTRODUCTION

THE LAND OF TUSCANY

AT the end of the third geological period the site of present-day Florence was covered by a lake. The sea, which had at first penetrated as far as Siena and Empoli, had since receded as the result of an upheaval of the earth's surface into new formations. In the fourth period this inland water was able to drain away to the sea and the deeper places which it had annexed came to form the course of the Arno today. However, this shallow depression stretching beyond Pistoia in the north-west is still cut off from the coast by the undulating terrain, and this has a considerable effect on the climate.

To the north-east stands a ring of hills, and beyond them are the Apennines whose vast folds and creases also date from the Tertiary. Though the peaks in this part of the chain are of moderate height, mostly between 4,000 and 5,000 feet, they are sometimes sheer and often grim of aspect. Old sandstone provides the dominant note, together with friable slaty rock which decomposes into patches of clayey soil here and there. Chestnut trees flourish on the sandstone, while on the hills nearest the city olives and vines are found up to a height of 2,000 feet.

Though the climate is Mediterranean in type, it is very different from that of Nice, say. The Tyrrhenian Sea is only about fifty miles away, but the influence of the land mass is already sufficient to cause marked differences in the weather. Extremes of temperature are characteristic. On average there are fourteen days of frost and four of snow during the

16

year, and even in March the north wind blowing from the Apennines can be keen and fierce. In contrast, the maximum day-time temperature in summer averages eighty-six degrees, whereas that of Bari, much further south, is only eighty-one. Summer, too, is the driest season. In winter mist often hangs over the valley. The prevailing winds switch from the east in the morning to the west in the evening, except in summer when the sea breezes predominate because of the high temperature inland.

The Arno is a typical Mediterranean river. Two-thirds of its 150-mile course have been completed by the time Florence is reached, and over that distance the river descends from an altitude of over 5,000 feet where it rises at Monte Falterona to 160 feet after its junction with the Sieve. Water is slow to drain from the alluvial soil of the Florentine basin, and for a long while this region was marshy. A weir was created

THE OLD MARKET PLACE

at Florence with the idea of making the Arno navigable to small craft, but it is continually necessary to dredge the bottom in order to prevent flooding. In fact the river eats away the upper valley and on its way through the city it carries along tons of silt. The violent storms that occur in the late summer can raise its level by between two feet and twelve feet in less than half a day.

This part of Tuscany is one of the most densely populated regions in Italy, the numbers reaching nearly 1,000 to the square mile. These vigorous and prolific people have so far shown little inclination to emigrate.

A kind of rural exodus in the thirteenth century first brought people to the city. Some hold the view that at the beginning of the fourteenth century, before the advent of the Black Death, there would have been up to 120,000 inhabitants. In 1561 their numbers had fallen to 59,000 and were to rise again only very gradually, reaching 100,000 just before the Unification of Italy. But from that time growth was rapid and continuous : 167,000 in 1871, 233,000 in 1911, 323,000 in 1936. This rate was maintained despite the war, and today some 400,000 people live in Florence. If outlying places like Rovezzano, Settignano and Bagno a Ripoli are included — as they are in the municipal registers — the number is nearer 420,000.

What led to the prosperity that these figures indicate ? For a long time the main cause was the position held by Florence as a world tourist centre, attracting hordes of foreign visitors, plus the important fact that the libraries, the celebrated university and the Military Geographical Institute make it the intellectual capital of Italy.

Then, too, the country round about is rich, though this is due to the unremitting toil of generations rather than to the quality of the land. Mixed farming is usual, concentrating on cereals such as maize, wheat

THE ARNO AND THE PONTE VECCHIO

and millet. Olive trees yielding a particularly fine oil and vines, with an occasional mulberry tree, are common features of the scenery, and fruit trees and vegetables are also cultivated on a wide scale. So the city, impinging as it does on both the valley and the mountains, is naturally a great agricultural market.

Florence is proud to be counted a centre of industry. One of the trolley-buses advertises its destination as 'Industrial Area'. Rifredi, the north-western quarter, is packed with factories. Like most towns of any size, the Tuscan capital has metallurgical industries, machine workshops and factories making optical instruments; but the chief activity is the manufacture of textiles — wool (of prime importance in early times), silk and velvet — soap, and now shoes. At Sesto there still exists the highly regarded porcelain industry founded by the Marchese Ginori in 1735, three

DANTE AND THE DIVINA COMMEDIA, BY DOMENICO DI FRANCESCO

years before Sèvres, on the lines of those established in Saxony and Austria. Nonetheless, one must be realistic. The recent efforts in the face of all obstacles to maintain enterprises which are no more than average are symptomatic of the times and conditions. It is unlikely that Florence will ever become a leading industrial city on a par with Milan, for instance. Apart from the fact that this region has no fuel except for lignite found near Arezzo, the supply of minerals is very limited.

The development of local crafts seems much more certain. For generations these have provided thousands of families with their livelihood. Even with the increasing export trade in straw goods, the ancient skills are still holding their own and more. Examples are embroidery, fine linen, bookbinding, stationery, high-quality leather goods, mosaic-work, stone and alabaster carvings, and superb jewellery.

Easy communications with Rome and Naples to the south and, by means of the long tunnel bored under the Apennines near the Passo della Porretta, with Milan and Bologna to the north, as well as with the near-by port of Leghorn, ensure that Florence today enjoys a commercial prosperity by no means unworthy of its great past.

HISTORICAL DEVELOPMENT

Precise information about Florence in ancient times is all but lacking. Although there is plenty of archaeological evidence proudly displayed in the museum in the Via della Colonna, written material is rare. Originally an Etruscan city, it was adopted by the Romans at an early date and Florus tells us that in Sulla's time

SELF-PORTRAIT: ANDREA DEL SARTO

SELF-PORTRAIT: FILIPPINO LIPPI

SELF-PORTRAIT : MICHELANGELO

it was considered one of the *municipia Italiae splendidissima*. The advantages of its situation on one of the chief roads, the Via Cassia, within easy reach of the sea, made it a prosperous agrarian settlement in the early years of the Empire. It was built in the form of a square, like the Roman camps, and the forum in the centre was near the present-day Piazza della Repubblica. The Via Roma and Via Calimala in one direction and the Via Strozzi and the Via del Corso in the other still follow the lines of the two main roads of Florence in the first century.

Christianity was undoubtedly established here in the third century; the first recorded Bishop of Florence lived in the reign of Constantine. In the dark and troubled times that followed, the city passed into shadow, emerging only briefly with the

ANONYMOUS PORTRAIT OF PETRARCH
(FOURTEENTH CENTURY)

LORENZO THE MAGNIFICENT :
DETAIL OF A FRESCO BY GHIRLANDAIO

resounding victory of Stilicho over the Goths at Fiesole in 406. Whether this decline was due to Attila's raiding bands, as Dante asserted (*Inferno*, XIII, 149), or to Totila in the next century, as Villani claimed, the fact remains that the appalling Gothic wars described by Procopius, together with the siege by Belisarius in 540, spread destruction here as everywhere in Italy; and under the Lombards Florence was heard of no more.

In the Carlovingian era, however, the city came back into prominence through a legend that quickly took root. According to this, it had been rebuilt and, indeed, founded anew by Charlemagne; and it may not have been far from the truth for his successors were patrons of Florence, helping to found abbeys such as the Badia a Ripoli (in 790) and schools, and promoting trade. This revival was short-lived, however. As early as the second half of the ninth century imperial rule was replaced by a Germanic dynasty of counts and the feudal system was firmly established. Lucca was where these governors of Tuscany chose to reside. The following century brought the terror of the Hungarian raids and a repetition of the disasters of 400 years before.

With the resurgence of the Empire, now in the German hands of Otto I, Florence was designated the capital of the

BOCCACCIO, BY ANDREA DEL CASTAGNO

Margraves of Tuscany and enjoyed material prosperity once more. Boniface of Canossa and his daughter Matilda (died 1115) projected their influence far beyond the valley of the Arno. The city's wealth is indicated by the consecration in 1059 of a baptistery that had been rebuilt and finely decorated, but that wealth was accompanied by much corruption. The higher orders of the Church were rotten with simony and against this a native of Florence, Giovanni (St John) Gualberto, led a victorious campaign with his monastic reforms that he drew up in the solitude of Vallombrosa. So Florence, like many other states in the twelfth century, witnessed a double regeneration: of Christianity, after the salutary reforms of Pope Gregory VII, and of an increasing economic life leading in turn to a sense of community.

It is not possible to say exactly when municipal government was introduced. Some self-governing institutions which emerged while Matilda was in power were already well established at the time of her death. This development was precipitated by the weakened state of the Empire during the War of the Investitures. The reins of government were then taken up by the wealthier citizens who promptly embarked on a policy of conquest, beginning with the destruction of Fiesole in 1125. Even Frederick Barbarossa could not halt the Florentines whose territory towards the end of that redoubtable Emperor's reign already extended to Empoli in the west and the Mugello in the north-east, from where they controlled the road to Bologna. Evidence of their growing power is found in the new town wall built in 1172 and taking in for the first time a portion of the left bank. It cannot be denied that Pisa at that time had become a dangerous rival through her maritime trade.

The Guelphs and the Ghibellines made their appearance at the beginning of the thirteenth century. The conflict between these two factions was inevitable and the murder on Easter Day 1215 of young Buondelmonti by the Amidei on the Ponte Vecchio merely kindled the flame. One might sum up their differences by describing the Ghibellines as ardent supporters of the Emperor and the Guelphs as defenders of the Pope's cause; but the issue was far more complex. It was undoubtedly a matter of family interests rather than political ideologies — which is why we today find it so difficult to comprehend the late middle ages in Italy.

Supported by Frederick II and later by his son Manfred, the Ghibelline cause in Florence depended on the nobles; the Guelphs, on the other hand, were assisting the lower classes to secure political power. The second group had their first victory when Frederick died in 1250, and then suffered a severe reverse at Montaperti in 1260 'when the waters of the Arbia ran red' (*Inferno*, X, 86). They emerged finally triumphant in 1266, after Charles of Anjou, brother of Louis IX of France, had conquered Naples in their name. Florence was torn by bitter fighting which flared up even in churches like Santa Trinità. The victors stripped several palaces belonging to Ghibelline families and confiscated their possessions. The *Parte Guelfa* (not to be confused with the Guelph party) which was set up to administer these properties became virtually a state within the state, having its own highly efficient organization and police force, and even a fortified palace still standing today in the similarly named piazza. The rich men of the *Parte* remained utterly opposed to all attempts at

VIA DELLA NINNA

arbitration between the two factions. It was this tense atmosphere that Dante and Giotto knew in their early years.

The Florentines continued their policy of aggressive leadership. Well satisfied with the resounding defeat of Pisa by the Genoese fleet in 1284, they crushed the Ghibelline city of Arezzo at the battle of Campaldino in 1289: a striking revenge for Montaperti. But the triumphs of this ruthless progress could not overshadow the political and social drama that was being enacted within the city itself. For Florence the period 1250-1340 was one of economic expansion; the strong and well-organized *Arti* (guilds) took advantage of this in their struggle for power.

In 1250 a premature attempt at government on a democratic basis had been made. Charles of Anjou substituted another system in favour of the nobles, but disagreement was rife among them and this left the way clear for the *Arti*. Since 1282 these had enjoyed some authority; their 'priors' controlled the citizens' affairs. But above all the Ordinances of Justice decreed in 1293 against a threat of reaction after Campaldino emphasized once more the democratic character of the Republic, while laws against the nobles grew in number. On the other hand, the seven major *Arti* (*popolo grasso*) were disturbed by the prospect of too rapid an advance on the part of the *popolo minuto* and endeavoured to check them by uniting with the aristocracy.

The city was now very prosperous. Work had begun in 1284 on a new enceinte enclosing a much larger area — of some 1,500 acres. The new town plan, moreover, was more ambitious, resulting in some vast open spaces, chiefly in the form of gardens. About the same time the foundations of most of Florence's famous monuments were laid, and Dante Alighieri wrote his immortal *Vita Nuova*.

More dissensions arose in 1300: the ruling class split up into White and Black Guelphs. The Blacks triumphed, with the aid of Pope Boniface VIII — fishing in troubled waters — and his French representative, the Comte de Valois. Among the Whites they drove out was Dante who for twenty years vented his unyielding hatred against his ungrateful native city for which he felt both love and loathing. From that time, as though in justification of his abuse, the decay of the Republic set in.

But this decay did not become apparent for fifty years. The growth of banking houses that handled the finances of all Europe, the undisputed primacy of the florin, the gold coin that had been struck in Florence since 1252, and the expansion of the wool industry still concealed the real facts. The ruling classes, now richer than ever, no longer encouraged the democratic movement. So tyranny emerged in Florence as in other parts of Italy.

A series of military defeats in the campaign against the Ghibelline lords Uguccione da Pisa and Castruccio Castracane brought humiliation on the Black Guelphs by forcing them to accept the embarrassing

HOUSE-FRONT IN THE BORGO S. IACOPO : ANNUNCIATION, BY DELLA ROBBIA

protectorship of a son of King Robert of Naples. Later, a series of calamities — more military reverses, the flood of 1333, and the resounding failure of the wealthy Peruzzi and Bardi banks — cast the Republic once more into the uncertainties of dictatorial rule. The new master was Walter de Brienne, Duke of Athens. It is true that his 'lifelong' rule lasted only from 8 September 1342 to 26 July 1343; owing his election to some malcontents who were unanimous in this purpose but no other, and above all to the common people, he turned everyone against him. The tyrant showed his rapacity and was ignominiously deposed.

Soon afterwards Florence, like all western Europe, was devastated by the Black Death. The subsequent changes in the numbers and distribution of population created a serious dislocation in the normal laws of supply and demand, wages and prices; and the social disorders which afflicted the city towards the end of the century stemmed in part from these causes.

After the fall of the Duke of Athens the trend towards democratic government resumed, and despite plenty of resistance the minor *Arti* managed to win power. Territorial expansion continued all the same — Pistoia, Prato and Volterra were all overrun. The arts, including literature, flourished more than ever. Petrarch had just finished his *Canzoni* and Boccaccio his *Decameron*, and the latter was also giving a course of lectures on the *Divina Commedia*. The Renaissance had arrived in a climax of intellectual activity.

On 20 July 1378 the Riot of the Ciompi (wool-carders) broke out. The most troublesome elements of the citizenry had been trying for thirty years to destroy the major *Arti* and had, moreover, been actively encouraged by the Duke of Athens. An erstwhile wool-carder turned adventurer, Michele di Lando, made use of this faction to carry out a bloodless revolution on that day which enabled him to take over the government in their name. Their triumph did not last a month. The middle classes, represented by the major *Arti*, took fresh heart at the perpetual complaints of the dissatisfied populus; the first shift in authority came in September and by 1382 the *popolo grasso* were back in command. The historian Rodolico has established that Michele performed a political *volte-face* — to his own financial advantage.

From 1382 to 1434 Florence was an oligarchy, chiefly in the hands of the ambitious Albizzi family. In external struggles the Republic met with some success but at a price. The Visconti of Milan and King Ladislas of Naples made dangerous adversaries. Still, Florence continued to extend its territory which by 1406 had reached the coast, through the annexation of that traditional rival, Pisa. In 1421 the city purchased the port of Leghorn from Genoa; the florin, obviously, was an all-powerful weapon.

The allegiance of the *popolo minuto*, plus their own political guile, enabled the enormously wealthy banking family of the Medici to join issue with the Albizzi. Rinaldo Albizzi scored an apparent victory when he forced Cosimo, the future 'Father of the City', into exile in 1433; but the latter was triumphantly recalled from Venice the following year to become ruler of Florence though no title was conferred upon him nor any alteration made to the republican statutes. This was the course that

Octavius had taken centuries before. The republic had become a principality.

Everyone knows how wonderful was the period that followed. Abroad, the city of the Lily, as successor to Pisa and rival to Venice, began to send her merchant ships to the Orient. At home, there were names to conjure with in every sphere of the arts : Leon Battista Alberti — universal wit, humanist and apostle of architectural harmony, Donatello, Marsilio Ficino, Politian, Lippi, Pico della Miràndola, Ghirlandaio, Botticelli, Vespucci.... They glorified that century as, too, did Lorenzo the Magnificent, grandson and successor of Cosimo il Vecchio, who governed from 1469 to 1492 and was patron of the arts, poet, military leader and accomplished statesman. That such a galaxy of great men could emerge in a couple of generations and in the same part of the world has never ceased to amaze posterity.

It must not be assumed that the Medici encountered no opposition to their rule. A conspiracy led by the Albizzi in 1440, some instability in the last years of Cosimo's reign, the brief but terrible rebellion of Volterra in 1472, and especially the dramatic events of 1478 show what a dangerous course the Medici had to steer. In 1478 a rival banking family, the Pazzi, hatched a cowardly plot — with the approval of Pope Sixtus IV — which was in the event abortive. Although Lorenzo's younger brother was killed, he himself escaped assassination by the conspirators. Popular indignation at that point was so extreme that it amounted to a plebiscite in favour of Lorenzo.

When he died at the age of forty-three in his villa at Careggi on 8 April 1492, Girolamo Savonarola, the monk from Ferrara, had been installed as Prior of San Marco for nearly three years. Moved by a truly prophetic spirit, he denounced the pagan depravity he beheld in the city; and his views were justified by such scandals as the elevation to the purple of one of Lorenzo's sons, not yet fourteen, by Pope Innocent VIII. Fra Girolamo foretold the advent of a conqueror who would wreak God's vengeance upon Florence.

Charles VIII of France did in fact make a triumphal entry into the city through the Porta San Frediano on 17 November 1494. Piero de' Medici had been forcèd to flee. For some months the new Republic submitted to Savonarola's dictatorship, but the temperament of this ascetic reformer made the citizens anxious to regain their liberty. The alliance with France cost them dear : in 1512 the Spanish troops of Julius II sacked Prato, thus forcing Florence to get rid of the Gonfaloniere Soderini and take as its master another of Lorenzo's sons, an ineffectual creature. The Cardinal de' Medici became Pope Leo X soon after this, and about the same time a Florentine diplomatist, Niccolò Machiavelli, was writing a short book, *Il Principe*, which was to attract some attention.

With yet another Medici on the papal throne, Clement VII, the position of the dynasty seemed unassailable. But when Charles V's troops under the leadership of the Constable of Bourbon seized Rome on 6 May 1527 and overthrew the Pope, revolt broke out in Florence and once again the Medici were deposed. Retaliation came quickly — the appalling siege of the city by the Emperor's armies during which Michelangelo fortified the campanile of San Miniato (1530). Having lost in dramatic circumstances the only great captain who could have saved it, Francesco Ferrucci, the city was taken. The Emperor presented it to the obnoxious Alessandro, a bastard of one of the Medici, who was later murdered by his cousin Lorenzino. His rule had the merit at least of removing all uncertainty: on 5 May 1532, in the Loggia de' Lanzi, the Republic came to an enforced end when the members of the *Signoria* yielded up their authority to Alessandro, now Duke of Tuscany.

In 1537 Cosimo I, son of the famous *condottiere* Giovanni delle Bande Nere, and distant cousin of Alessandro, acceded to the dukedom at the age of eighteen. He brought a certain distinction to Florence, acquired Siena during the Franco-Spanish wars, and finally obtained the title of grand duke from the Pope. For exactly 200 years the city was ruled by Cosimo's descendants.

For all its habitual pomp and splendour, the marriages with ancient royal houses (two of its daughters became queens of France), and the patronage it extended to scholars, this dynasty was completely unable to save Florence from decline, and the final blow was a ghastly epidemic

in 1630. The later history of the city seems infected with the utter mediocrity of subsequent rulers, on a par with the Habsburgs in Spain in their oscillations between superstitious piety and the most vicious crimes.

Painters no longer came to Florence to learn and perfect their art. Nevertheless it was here that, under the protection of one of the grand dukes, Galileo was able in his later years to spread the light of his knowledge. He died on 8 January 1642 in a villa at Pian de' Giullari. Great men, however, were now very rare in this city from which so many had sprung.

Cosimo III married a princess of Orléans who was mentally abnormal, and for the fifty-three years of his reign he watched, powerless, the long death-scene of his house. The last of the Medici was his only son, the debauched Gian Gastone (1723-37). The title was then conferred upon Francis, Duke of Lorraine, husband of Maria Theresa and founder of the house of Habsburg-Lorraine, who left his former estates to Stanislaus Leszczynski. His accession is commemorated by a high-flown inscription on a triumphal arch by the Lorraine sculptor Jadod in the present-day Piazza della Libertà.

This proud city showed neither affection nor dislike for the Austrian archdukes thus foisted upon it, and in fact theirs was a benevolent rule. It was due to the Archduke Peter Leopold who succeeded in 1765 that Tuscany was the first state to lift the

'CARROZZELLE'

31

restrictions on the corn trade. By the time he became Emperor of Austria in 1790 Florence was indebted to him for such benefits as agricultural reform, universal taxation, the abolition of the death penalty and a higher standard of education.

Soon after his departure came the repercussions from events in revolutionary and imperial France. On 30 June 1796 General Bonaparte entered Florence through the same gate as Charles VIII 300 years before. The Grand Duke had taken refuge at the Viennese Court, so his estates were used by the French as a means of barter. By the Treaty of Lunéville (1801) the First Consul made them into the 'Kingdom of Etruria' — neo-classicism was much in vogue — for the dispossessed Duke of Parma. The blockade of the Continent later furnished Napoleon (now Emperor) with a pretext for taking over the kingdom to which he sent his sister, Elisa Baciocchi, as his deputy. Following the tradition of royal patronage, she commissioned the interior decoration of the Palazzo Pitti and founded the Cherubini Musical Institute.

The Congress of Vienna restored Tuscany to the Habsburgs, of course, and life went on again as though nothing had happened. At least, that was what Metternich would have wished; but the libertarian principles proclaimed by France were finding support everywhere.

In Florence too liberal ideas, together with a vague desire for unity and increasing scorn for the Austrians and their language, brought the *Risorgimento* nearer. Nothing was actually done, however. While the rest of the country was periodically rocked by revolutionary disturbances and counteraction by the police, Florence remained calm. Even in 1848 there was much less violence here than elsewhere in Italy. Leopold II was deposed and had to flee to Gaeta, despite his earlier consent to the freedom of the press and, later, to a constitution. However, the provisional government of Guerrazzi soon collapsed (11 April 1849) and the sovereign was recalled.

The decisive hour for Florence and all Italy arrived in 1859. On 16 August the deposition of the House of Lorraine was proclaimed at the Palazzo Vecchio — the Archduke had in fact fled at the beginning of the Austro-Sardinian war. Bettino Ricasoli's government held a plebiscite on the proposed affiliation to Piedmont which was accordingly ratified on 25 March 1860. Italy became a kingdom the following year, and in 1865 Florence was made its capital as a result of the September Convention which sought to quieten Napoleon III's uneasiness in regard to Rome. For six years Victor Emmanuel II resided in the city, at either the Palazzo Pitti or the Villa della Petraia, which he preferred; so until 1871 Florence was a centre of affairs like any other great European capital.

Tranquil detachment pervaded the city in its most prosperous phase at the turn of the century; a calm that was for some time barely ruffled by the echoes of the Great War. The Florentines were mainly indifferent to Fascism, even though Mussolini had written, not without irony, in the city's Golden Book while on a visit there : '*A Firenze fascistissima!*' He must have been well aware that dozens of witticisms and caustic comments on the regime that were current in Italy had originated in this very town, the most censorious of them all. When Hitler passed through here in the spring of 1938, he was received with elegance and even splendour, but no enthusiasm.

The civilized world stirred with uneasiness in 1944 when, after the capture of Rome, Florence moved into the line of fire. The German command ordered all the bridges to be blown up with the exception of the Ponte Vecchio, which Hitler had admired. The streets leading to the mediaeval bridge, Via de' Guicciardini and Via Por Santa Maria, were destroyed, after evacuation, in order to check the advance of the Allied armies. The latter entered Florence by the Porta Romana on 11 August and were joined by groups of partisans who had come down from the mountains.

The problems of social order became more and more acute for the city council trying to deal with the difficulties of reconstruction and traffic congestion which was getting worse each year, as much for pedestrians during rush hours as for motorists all the time. In 1951 a professor of Roman law at the University, a little Sicilian with an unforgettable smile, was appointed chief magistrate. In the course of his first eight years at the Palazzo Vecchio the Sindaco Giorgio La Pira was not only the protector of the poor, the destitute and the unemployed — to the horror of mere economists. He instituted the Florence Congresses for peace and Christian civilization, and the Meeting of mayors from principal towns throughout the world. A pilgrim of peace, he had a keen sense of the significance of his city in times to come. Strongly religious, he meditated upon the meaning of cities, their role in history, and the vital necessity of peace in an atomic world. It was because Florence exists and because he loved it that in 1954 he demanded in the presence of the International Red Cross Committee that 'the inviolable character of certain places and zones that are essential for the very existence of human civilization' should be recognized.

He expressed what we all feel. 'My Florence, calm and harmonious and moderate, created, so to speak, by both man and God to be, like the city on the mountain, a source of light and reassurance to us on our way, Florence does not want to die.... Cities have a life of their own; they have a being of their own, secret and profound. They have each a face, they have each, as it were, a soul and a destiny. They are not occasional heaps of stones. They are mysterious habitations of men and still more, in a certain way, mysterious habitations of God.'

THE PEOPLE OF FLORENCE. FESTIVALS AND TRADITIONS

In this melting-pot of races that was Italy it is hardly possible to discern the basic physical character of each of them. The slanted eyes

THE MARKET OF SAN LORENZO

and malicious grin of the Etruscans have not become particularly characteristic of Florentine faces.

Yet in a country so conscious of local distinctions the personality
of each province contrasts sharply with the others. A Florentine could
never be mistaken for a Milanese, a Roman or a Neapolitan. Look about
you in the streets, where at any moment may appear Botticelli's *Man
with a Medal*, or the unknown *Old Man* painted by Lippi, or Verrocchio's
youthful *David*. Among all these different faces the most typical one is
basically serious with intelligent eyes and a firm mouth that is quick to

retort, to give a plain answer or a caustic reply. The women are slender, even graceful, and undoubtedly resemble the three Graces of Botticelli's *Primavera* more than Michelangelo's sombre *Night*.

So the faces that we see reflect the character of these men and women stamped by the past and the present of their remarkable city. An intense love of freedom — but freedom of speech, perhaps, rather than action. A critical attitude allied to unusual mental flexibility and an artistic sense that is entirely spontaneous. Not for nothing have generations of these citizens lived in the constant presence of great masterpieces and their small daughters played hide-and-seek behind the water-clad nymphs of the *Biancone* fountain. The poorest tramp is at liberty here to spend hours day-dreaming in the shadow of Cellini's *Perseus*. This perpetual and close contact with beautiful things accounts for the most striking characteristic of the man in the street here. He is conscious of beauty, he absorbs it, savours it, feels it; more than that, he can talk about it.

Intellect is accorded universal respect, and not just in academic circles. The tide of materialism is less apparent here than in other places. Old Florentine families are simple, even austere, in their mode of life, able to do without central heating in the winter, and to be satisfied with frugal meals. Television is very popular, however, and the panorama of red-tiled roofs is marred by the antennae of innumerable aerials. Extreme trends of thought are found. At present Communism is keenly supported in the working-class areas. Due recognition, too, must be given to the initiative in social matters taken by a small Catholic group who do indeed practise their Christianity : La Pira is not alone. In the heedless mob the tendency to criticize is often accompanied by a degree of unreasoning and superficial antagonism towards the clergy. The Florentine is still the *enfant terrible* of Italy.

The man in the street is affable but reserved with strangers, though if invited he will not hesitate to give his comments on a play or the latest news. In his speech certain sounds are oddly aspirated, and he will talk glowingly of Giotto's *hhampanile*. He can explain his traditions and the festivals he is so proud of; and he takes part in these with an exuberant vitality which quite overshadows the folk-lore aspect.

The *scoppio del carro*, part of the Easter ceremonies, is held at midday on Easter Sunday in the Piazza del Duomo. The whole city takes an interest in it. '*E andata bene, la colombina ?*' — 'The dove did its job all right ?' the ones who could not be at the *scoppio* ask dejectedly. An imitation dove is sent gliding along a wire from the cathedral choir to ignite the fireworks placed in a superbly decorated chariot drawn by white oxen to a position between the Baptistery and the cathedral steps. The next five minutes is the *scoppio*, a dreadful racket when one is on top of it. It is believed to commemorate the fire which, according to pilgrims and crusaders in the eleventh century, was seen to spring from the lamps

in the Holy Sepulchre on Easter Saturday. If the fireworks are successfully exploded, a good harvest is forecast.

As it seems more like a historical reconstruction, the *Calcio*, which takes place in the Piazza della Signoria on St John's Day (the city's festival), deserves to be seen. The game, apparently a fore-runner of football, is played in fifteenth-century costume — a brilliant medley of colours — and is preceded by an imposing procession of the *Signoria*.

But the most characteristic and the most ancient of these traditions is undoubtedly the cricket hunt on Ascension Day, last sign of the rejoicings, the *maggiolate*, which once marked the month of spring itself. On this Thursday children and teenagers set off early for the Cascine to rout out the singing insects from their underground nests. They spend the whole day there, eat lunch on the grass, dance and play and generally enjoy themselves. For the next week or so the town is full of pedlars hawking miniature cages, each with its tiny black prisoner. In some local

1.

2.

festivities there still survives a strong and genuine popular tradition. But the *rificolone*, the paper lanterns which used to be carried in procession on 7 September, the vigil of the Virgin's Nativity, and a joy in the days when the streets were still unlit, are seen less and less.

3.

4.

5.

CRAFTSMEN AT WORK. 1, 2, 3 : GILDED LEATHER-WORK. 4, 5 : WORKING IN STONE

THE PHARMACIST IN THE TRECENTO : BASE OF THE CAMPANILE

In a city where music has always been held in high esteem it is not surprising that the public is admitted free to the excellent concerts given in the Sala dei Dugento (Palazzo Vecchio); and working people from Santa Croce mingle with wealthy residents of the Via Bolognese in the audience. A splendid gesture on the part of the municipal authorities which has since been copied at Bologna.

The *Maggio Musicale*, which was inaugurated before the war, is appreciated as much by Florentine society as by visitors staying in Tuscany. This 'May of Music' actually continues well into July. For two glorious months concerts and operas are held at the Teatro della Pergola, the

Teatro Comunale, the Palazzo Vecchio, and in the Giardino di Boboli. Quite recently a bold attempt was made to stage *Die Walküre* here. It made a strange, unreal picture on the lawns with the hill behind, and the music, alas, was ruined. I still remember and marvel at a Shakespearean production that was performed alongside the Palazzo Pitti, just by the gardens. The massed shadows of the trees and a light sky sparkling with stars completed the scene, while the crickets in the flower-beds and the occasional sound of a near-by monastery bell tolling its prayer in the warm summer night provided the most discreet and apt accompaniment to the glorious lines and the subtle and elegant performance of the Italian actors.

But Florence does not belong to just one season. The palaces whose fierce beauty was softened by the summer light resume their cold dignity in the depths of winter. The formidable outlines of the Palazzo Strozzi and the Palazzo Vecchio look very well in a slight mist. This more austere guise, in fact, may well reveal the essential character of the city.

THE LILY OF FLORENCE :
MEDALLION ON ORSANMICHELE

THE ROAD UP TO FIESOLE

FROM THE TOP OF FIESOLE

PRELUDE AT FIESOLE

For our purpose, the time to climb up to Fiesole is early in the morning before the sun is too high in the sky, for the light is at its best at about ten o'clock. The spectacle is no less fine in the afternoon but the hazy atmosphere obscures the view; cupolas and campaniles are indistinct, while further down the winding Arno glides along here, disappears there, like fragments of a silver mirror. That is the hour for the thinker, the poet. The historian, who demands precision, will choose the morning for his visit.

Naturally the climb must be made on foot — forget the trolley-bus. To appreciate the charm of this place, one must be free to linger now and then, look at the vines and the olive trees which cloak the hill, dawdle where the walls of an attractive villa cast their shade over the road, turn occasionally to see how much further the view now extends. Or even sit down on a milestone and reread one of the tales of the *Decameron*; for it was the park of the Villa Palmieri right below Fiesole that Boccaccio made the setting of his stories as they were told in turn by seven ladies and three gentlemen who had fled from the city at the time of the plague. An inscription on the entrance of the Villa Albizzi reads: 'These walls have witnessed the songs, poems and dances of the Accademia dei Generosi. A masterly production of Giovanni Paisiello's *The Chinese Idol* was given here in the autumn of 1775.... In those more elegant times the ascent of this pleasant hill was harder than it is today, but the welcome was more gracious and the entertainment more lively.'

The passer-by finds many such reminiscences on his way.

For the citizen of Florence it is a moving experience to go up to Fiesole, the home of his forbears. Dante constantly recalls the fact that the Florentines had their origin up there. The stiff-necked people he abused had something of 'the mountain and the rock' in their nature (*Inferno*, XV, 61-63). Brought up and living in the plain, he was ever conscious of where his roots lay.

The people of Florence are obviously proud of their descent from Caesar's colonists, but they are connected with the Etruscan inhabitants

FIESOLE : THE ROMAN THEATRE

FIESOLE : THE CAMPANILE

of *Faesulae* too. Giovanni Villani wrote: 'Observe, reader, that there is no cause for surprise in the fact that the Florentines are in a perpetual state of war or internal conflict, for their ancestors were opposed in their customs and always at enmity: the brave Romans on one side, and the uncouth, boisterous warriors of Fiesole on the other.'

43

San Domenico is the first stopping-place. Not that there is much of interest inside this Dominican monastery, but the chapter-house has a fresco by Fra Angelico, otherwise known as Giovanni da Fiesole. He and the archbishop St Antoninus, his contemporary, took their vows here. The principal feature of the monastery is its wonderful situation, half-way between the city and Fiesole. A few minutes' walk brings one down to the Badia Fiesolana, Fiesole's original cathedral, with an admirable Romanesque façade overlooking the Mugnone valley. On the other side paths lead one gently down below Monte Ceceri where in 1505 Leonardo da Vinci is said to have made his famous and still mysterious aeronautical experiment. Further on, in the direction of Maiano and

FIESOLE : FAÇADE OF THE BADIA

FIESOLE : ENTRANCE TO SAN FRANCESCO

Vincigliata, these paths run past villas with white walls and green shutters, or little country houses like the one where Temple Leader wrote his biography of the *condottiere* Sir John Hawkwood.

Resuming the ascent from San Domenico, one reaches the centre of Fiesole in twenty minutes. The interior of the unpretentious cathedral has great purity of style, and its Romanesque choir is raised, like those of San Miniato in Florence and St-Hilaire in Poitiers. The battlemented campanile can be seen from afar, outlined against the sky in the sort of saddle where the town is clustered. The fragile grace of this tower is

45

enchanting and disturbing to see. In addition to the small and peaceable community of peasants and artisans turning out woven straw goods, the Bishop of Fiesole has in his care a cosmopolitan society. Scattered about the hillside, like a park in itself, are several cheerful villas owned in some cases by Florentines but in many others by foreigners, particularly British people.

A broad-flagged street leads off the main square and climbs and winds its way up to the highest point of the hill. What a view ! A thousand feet below Florence spreads its riches in scornful indifference to its fallen ancestor. The little monastery of San Francesco has stood since 1352 on the Etruscan acropolis, and its soothing calm has appealed to many pilgrims. Though the tiny cloister is cut off from the panorama outside, it offers the surprise of a dazzling carpet of flowers beneath a chunk of sky; one of the cells belonged to St Bernardine of Siena. Some primitives are to be found in the unassuming church.

Going down again towards the Duomo, walk round the apse. Below the campanile lie the curving grey tiers of Sulla's theatre, excavated many years ago. The grassy stage is occasionally used for revivals of Plautus, with an unexpected landscape providing the back-drop. We are at the back of the hill, above the valley of the Mugnone — a complete change of scene : the distant hills of the Mugello have an air of austerity. In this utterly restful spot one can, too, explore the ruins of the baths and the temple which have recently been brought to light. The Romans, who had burnt down the original temple, rebuilt it with a carved pediment of terracotta in the Etruscan manner. Impressive fragments of the walls are still standing. Though lacking the wonderful proportions of the gate at Perugia, these magnificent remains are fully deserving of attention as the sole legacy of a people who are still an enigma. Later, when strolling through *Florentia*, the first impact of the Palazzo Strozzi will call to mind Mauclair's assertion that the principles of Etruscan architecture 'haunted the builders of the old Florentine palaces' and that Fiesole was the fore-runner of Florence.

RIPE CORN IN THE SUNLIGHT

PIAZZA DELLA SIGNORIA

ENTRANCE TO THE PALAZZO VECCHIO

THE HEART OF THE CITY

Piazza del Duomo! Piazza della Signoria! These are, respectively, the religious and political centres of the old Guelph city. World-famous, both, but differently affected by the tide of modern life.

The road down from Fiesole leads abruptly into the Piazza del Duomo by way of the Via de' Martelli. In the early dawn this is a place of marble,

THE DUOMO, CAMPANILE AND BAPTISTERY

the throbbing din of bells, and the beat of birds' wings; but the focus of a deafening uproar and an inferno of traffic beneath the web of overhead cables in the rush hours, particularly between six and eight in the evening. So dense then is the human tide that it is difficult to arrange a rendezvous, unless one stands at the corner of the Loggia del Bigallo near the policeman who, from his Olympian position on top of some steps, endeavours to direct pedestrians across the road with peremptory blasts on his whistle.

So one must be prepared to come here very early to enjoy in relative peace this unique group of monuments comprising the huge vermilion dome which stresses cathedral and city alike, the Campanile and the Baptistery. Facing the overpowering Duomo (Santa Maria del Fiore) and near the Campanile — one's first sight of this is unforgettable — and older than both of these, the octagonal Baptistery with its dark-green and white marble seems wholly adapted to this setting, though it was built for a completely different ensemble. Its proportions and the classical purity of its lines create an impression of perfect balance. Whatever its early origins, San Giovanni as it is today cannot be called a temple of Mars or a Christian foundation of the Lombard queen, Theodolinda. These walls date from the eleventh century, when it was still the cathedral; later, in 1128, the episcopal see was transferred to Santa Reparata

THE BAPTISTERY : NORTH DOOR

EAST DOOR: THE CREATION OF ADAM AND EVE, BY GHIBERTI

SOUTH DOOR: THE BURIAL OF
ST JOHN THE BAPTIST, BY ANDREA PISANO

NORTH DOOR:
THE TEMPTATION, BY GHIBERTI

as a result of the increase in population. Each century added to its beauty, and Dante in exile dwelt nostalgically upon '*il mio bello San Giovanni*'.

Leaving the famous bronze doors for examination later, let us go inside, passing between antique sarcophagi of which one at least was in the collection belonging to Lorenzo de' Medici. The magnificent thirteenth-century mosaics, partly Byzantine, which cover the apse and cupola call to mind St Mark's in Venice. For the first time those in the cupola can be seen clearly thanks to an excellent lighting system which has now been installed. The mosaics in the apse are older, the work of a Minorite friar at the time of St Francis, in 1225. The role of the patron saint in this city is shown by the portrayal of him here, seated opposite the Virgin. Part of the ancient pavement of inlaid marble is still visible, with the original inscriptions. Half in shadow is the tomb of Cardinal Cossa (the Antipope John XXIII), the work of Donatello and Michelozzo.

A strange statue stands near the door. If the men of those times loved life with a pagan intensity, they undoubtedly had a deep-rooted sense of sin nonetheless. In the fifteenth century that contrast was present in Florence as everywhere else. Anticipating the menaces of Savonarola, Donatello made this wood-carving of Mary Magdalene, a truly hideous figure which Charles VIII vainly demanded from the Florentines. The long tresses which were once her glory among the Galileans cover only withered flesh. This is the recluse of the Blessed Grotto, an emaciated penitent transfigured by her tears. 'She has given me an everlasting aversion for penitence,' was the gentle comment of De Brosses. This very since-rity is a great tribute to the sculptor's power of expression.

It is probably common knowledge that Michelangelo declared the door on the east side of the Baptistery to be worthy of Paradise. It is later than those on the north and south sides which mark equally important stages in the history of Tuscan sculpture. These six leaves, which were removed during the war, are better known than ever since an ingenious (and cautious) technician succeeded in dissolving the thick crust of soli-dified dust combined with verdigris that masked them; all he used was caustic soda. So the gilt facing of these reliefs can be seen again in all its splendour, unchanged after five centuries.

For the south door, by which we entered, Andrea Pisano did the original relief depicting the life of St John the Baptist in 1330, and this was finished in 1336. Though he still followed the Gothic formulas of the Pisan school, Giotto's influence saved him from its mannerism; that master's touch is noticeable in the draperies of the figures and the simpli-city and vigour of the modelling.

The north door was the result of the famous competition of 1402. The winner, Lorenzo Ghiberti, defeated six illustrious rivals. He was twenty-four at the time and spent more than twenty years on the casting of this door, which was hung in 1424. Almost immediately he began

EAST DOOR OR 'GATE OF PARADISE' : SCENES FROM THE OLD TESTAMENT, BY GHIBERTI

NORTH SIDE : THE MASS

WEST SIDE : THE DRUNKENNESS OF NOAH

work on the one for the east side, and this occupied him, aided by a galaxy of pupils, until his death. The northern leaves reveal a mediaeval inspiration still, with their twenty-eight quatrefoils in the same scale as the previous ones. At the bottom are evangelists and teachers, and above them the work of the Redeemer is portrayed. Ghiberti's style at this stage was characterized by a touching restraint, a lively and creative harmony which was, however, rigidly controlled. With the words: 'Thou shalt worship the Lord thy God', Christ in the wilderness overwhelms Satan, and his sorcerer's wings droop towards the ground, where the stones have not been changed into bread. There is no unnecessary word or syllable in this account.

But on the east door, some twenty years later in date, *mira arte fabricatum*, the scenes from the Old Testament confront us with the Renaissance at its height. Ten pictures in relief, entirely covered with gilt, tell the story of the Chosen People from Eve to Solomon. The sense of rhythm is still there. But in the new consciousness of spatial relations (the magnificent columns of Isaac's house, the section of Solomon's palace, the depth in the panorama of Jericho), the manifold scenes comprising each panel, and the luxuriant borders with their profusion of spring flowers and familiar creatures like partridges, goldfinches and squirrels — in all this is reflected the city of the Medici, with its passionate interest in man and nature and sheer intoxication with form.

Regretfully we turn away to study the Duomo. It is best to ignore

THE CAMPANILE : EAST SIDE

the modern façade with its meaningless and excessive decoration and assess the church by its interior. A sombre bareness here. 'Caught between mediaeval and classical taste,' wrote Taine, 'between coloured and clear light, the architect achieved only a wan and lifeless effect.' The pure Gothic arches soar from fourteenth-century pillars. The utter emptiness of this cathedral never fails to astonish. One is immediately struck by both the vastness and the perfect proportions of the endless nave with its three aisles; by the austerity and, too, the tonal quality of the *pietra serena*, the local grey stone with its inimitable texture which is to be seen everywhere in Florence. Brunelleschi's dome, the largest in the world after St Peter's, towers 300 feet over the choir, presenting Zuccari's fresco of *The Last Judgment* to the awestruck sightseer.

The new cathedral was begun in 1296, to replace Santa Reparata; in 1436

DONATELLO : 'LO ZUCCONE'

THE DUOMO : UNFINISHED PIETÀ, BY MICHELANGELO

it was consecrated in the name of the Virgin Mary by Pope Eugenius IV. Such were the crowds that, according to a complacent inscription on a marble slab, a wooden footway from Santa Maria Novella had to be constructed for the pontifical procession. In 1439 the famous Council of Florence proclaimed here, in the presence of the eastern Emperor John Palaeologus, the short-lived union of the Roman and Greek Churches. Here, too, the hired assassins of the Pazzi murdered Giuliano de' Medici. Later, Savonarola thundered out his harsh warnings within these walls. Under this impressive dome have come and gone the soldiers of Charles VIII, the Emperor Charles V, Eugène de Beauharnais and General (now Lord) Alexander. Yet it remains *dum volvitur urbis*.

MUSEO DELL' OPERA DEL DUOMO :
ST JOHN THE EVANGELIST, BY DONATELLO

Beneath the cupola the vast, dim octagonal choir is dominated by the great crucifix of Benedetto da Maiano. The three apses round it, with their numerous chapels, are plunged in semi-darkness, though this has been relieved somewhat since the stained-glass windows were cleaned — which represent the work of the most celebrated masters of Renaissance Florence. The space, the echoing pavement and the blank walls create a chilling atmosphere. Those accustomed to the French Gothic style find it difficult to appreciate these overwhelming masses. Prayer seems to have no place here. Nevertheless it is the key to the city itself. The Florentine character, with its majesty, its Dantesque sense of tragedy and its sombre dignity, is cast in the image of the Duomo.

Luca della Robbia's lunettes of the *Resurrection* and the *Ascension* over the doors of the two sacristies bring visual relief for a moment, with their guileless blues. Elsewhere, triumphal figures adorn the walls. A *Dante* by Domenico di Michelino indicates the three realms he has passed through; two great *condottieri* in monochrome imitating sculpture, huge and cumbersome figures, were executed by Uccello and Andrea del Castagno.

This cathedral has many associations with Michelangelo : he modelled the dome of St Peter's on this one. But he is chiefly represented by the

MUSEO DELL' OPERA DEL DUOMO : 'CANTORIA', BY DONATELLO

Pietà, done in his eightieth year. Unfinished, like so many other works of his, filled with desolation, the group is designed around the limp body of Christ between the tender, poignant silence of Mary and the more theatrical sorrow of the Magdalene. Like the shadow of some graveyard cypress Nicodemus raises his cowled head, and in the utter disillusion of his expression it is easy to identify the master himself.

The delightful north and south doors should not be overlooked. The Portale della Mandorla illustrates the transition from mediaeval to Renaissance design in the early fifteenth century. The Portale dei Canonici, older and more restrained, follows the Italian Romanesque tradition. Outside once more, all feeling of oppression vanishes; the triumphal contrasts of Giotto's Campanile and the cathedral dome together proclaim the glory of God and the hope of the world.

Of the pair Florence is probably more attached to the Campanile, but these two marvels are indivisible. It is impossible to imagine one without the other, any more than a peach without its stone or Paolo

'IL CUPOLONE'

apart from Francesca. Look at them again together, from the corner of the Via de' Pecori, for a better perspective; the sleek, slender tower seems a prop for Brunelleschi's marvellous half-sphere.

The Campanile is virtually the last will and testament of Giotto di Bondone, who began it in 1334 but died a couple of years later, leaving it unfinished. Talenti completed it in the second half of the century, after the terrible interruption of the Black Death. The unity of style is explained by the relative speed with which it was built. In it is expressed that genius for 'regularity of form and harmony of proportions' that, says Focillon, Tuscany presented in opposition to the Gothic style infiltrating from France, even though the latter left its mark in the perfect *bifore*. These tall coupled windows are dominated by one immense *trifora* in the top storey. This great four-cornered tower sweeps up to a height of 292 feet, and every detail of its design, from the unobtrusive colouring of its marbles to the composition of its forms and relief, gives delight. Masterly carvings decorate the lower parts, though it is difficult to see the development in its entirety since the second series of reliefs in their lozenge-shaped cartouches is already too far above ground level. But patient examination reveals the theme : how Man, from the time of his creation — the wonderful Eve emerging from the hands of God is reminiscent of carvings at Orvieto — first conceived the arts and sciences essential to his needs. Pastoral life and metallurgy are signified respectively by Tubalcain and Noah... after the vintage. Then came more sophisticated discoveries including social justice as well as astronomy and the art of flying (Daedalus), sculpture (Phidias) and painting (Apelles). Higher up, the pupils of Andrea Pisano depicted the seven planets which govern human affairs juxtaposed with the seven liberal arts, the seven virtues and the seven sacraments by which men come to God. How typical of the *trecento*, which could treat these parallel allegories with equal respect.

From the corner of the Via dell' Oriuolo, look again at Brunelleschi's masterpiece. It is certainly not without fault. Some regard it as a colossal monstrosity, while others are shocked by the discrepancy between the plebeian russet tiles and the aristocratic white marble ribs that meet at the lantern which, topped by a ball and cross, looks like the tiara of some oriental potentate. It is regrettable that the graceful gallery running along one section of the drum has never been completed because of Michelangelo's sarcastic comment that it looked like a cage for grasshoppers. Despite such criticisms, however, even the most exacting eye cannot be indifferent to the fine proportions of the massive dome or fail to find deep satisfaction in its perfect lines.

Close to the apse of this celebrated basilica is the Museo dell' Opera del Duomo, which was rearranged not long ago and is certainly worth a visit. It contains some fourteenth-century statues of the apostles and

ORSANMICHELE

evangelists which were intended for the façade, and at one time several of them were set up in the aisles of the Duomo, including Donatello's fine *St John the Evangelist* which must have influenced Michelangelo's *Moses*. The originals of the sixteen prophets, patriarchs and sibyls on the Campanile, much damaged by the elements in the course of 500 years, have also been brought here for safety. For the first time they can be seen properly. Examples are Donatello's remarkably ugly *Jeremiah* and his *Habakkuk*, popularly nicknamed *Lo Zuccone* (pumpkin) on account of his long bald head. But what draws the public here is the two well-known and much photographed choir-gallery parapets.

These *cantorie* were carved respectively by Donatello and Luca della Robbia at about the same time (1435), and until 1688 they were set above the sacristy doors in the Duomo. Like the statues of the prophets, these are seen to much better advantage here, sad though it is when a work of art is deprived of the setting for which it was designed. Donatello's graceful little pagans of *putti* dance with wild frenzy, creating, according to Lavedan, 'a confusion of lines dominated by diagonals which hints at the baroque'. Luca's version opposite demonstrates a more Attic conception of beauty. The intense effort of the choir, the vibrant trumpets held aloft, the graceful movements of the naked young singers, the girls skipping in a ring — in all this is expressed that particular rapture of the spirit extolled by the prophet in the 150th Psalm; for

ANDREA DELLA ROBBIA :
EMBLEM OF THE SILK-WEAVERS

VERROCCHIO :
THE INCREDULITY OF ST THOMAS

this was the very text that the sculptor had been commissioned to illustrate. His interpretation is curiously touching, and never loses its effect.

Returning to the Campanile, we shall take the Via dei Calzaiuoli which leads into the Piazza della Signoria. There one may be greeted by the sight of two men in unusual dress. They are not members of one of those pious but flamboyant brotherhoods, to be found in Italy as in Corsica, who wear a red or bright blue hood over a white or brown cassock and may be seen on feast days marching behind their great processional figures of Christ draped in purple. Indeed no. These grey-robed men are two circumspect brothers of the *Misericordia* returning from an errand of mercy to their headquarters near the Campanile. (In their chapel is a *St Sebastian* by Benedetto da Maiano.) Aristocrat and artisan, lawyer and *vetturino* are all on equal terms in this organization; social barriers in Tuscany are in any case less rigid than elsewhere in Italy. The fraternity was founded in 1240 or thereabouts by one Andrea Gallerani of Siena; by the beginning of the fifteenth century it was already of some consequence in the city. Today these men still look after the poor and sick, arranging urgent treatment and transport to hospital. Their modern equipment includes an X-ray unit and excellent noiseless ambulances which have been paid for by voluntary subscriptions from all over the world — even from Italians in Brazil. Until a relatively short time ago each man wore his hood over his face to preserve his anonymity, and occasionally the passer-by would be nabbed at the corner of the street by a mendicant brother with his square alms box on the end of a staff. Or at dusk one might pass the funeral procession of some poor soul being taken to his last resting-place by the *Misericordia*, making their way quickly through the tortuous streets by the light of their smoking torches.

Right on the corner of the Via dei Calzaiuoli stands the Loggia del Bigallo, built in the middle of the fourteenth century and originally the seat of the confraternity of that name. Abandoned infants used to be put on view beneath the porch. Its small statues, including an ungainly but attractive madonna, wrought-iron grille from Siena, *bifore* and twisted columns are typically elegant examples of Tuscan art in the *trecento*.

If it is not too crowded, turn now into the Via dei Calzaiuoli, a very busy and lively street. Passing the corner of the Via degli Speziali one can see to the right an extremely ugly triumphal arch, dating from the last century, beyond the vast Piazza della Repubblica where café tables may be set out on the pavements. Continuing on our way, which takes us past some elegant and very tempting shop windows, we reach, a few yards further on, the massive cube of Orsanmichele (San Michele in Orto).

Only a little later in date than the Campanile and the Loggia del Bigallo (1404), this was originally a kind of granary; corn was stored

THE PALAZZO VECCHIO

here against the constant possibility of a siege or in case of famine. When such stocks were increased later on, the ground floor was converted into a chapel. The municipal council, it is recorded in the minutes, wanted something 'of the utmost splendour and magnificence'. From the beginning of the fifteenth century the walls were sumptuously decorated with a series of canopied niches, all different, set on either side of the great blind bays — note the superb ornament — of the one-time loggia. In the corner-stones below the windows of the upper hall are large medallions in faience bearing the colourful coats of arms of the guilds. All this was commissioned by the *Arti*. One of the most original features of Renaissance Florence was perhaps the fact that the arts owed their continuance not to an old and decadent aristocracy but to these all-powerful industrial or financial organizations, or families who took a leading part in them. Bankers whose interests extended all over Europe, money-changers, weavers, mercers and dyers — all were anxious to show off their wealth, their sophisticated culture and their orthodox beliefs; and this very ostentation must be allowed the credit for many artists and many unique masterpieces.

Beneath the pinnacles or pediments of the fourteen niches the *Arti* set statues of their patron saints. The present *St George*, patron of the armourers, is only a copy of Donatello's work which has been transferred to the Bargello. Vasari praised the statue for its quality of calm and resolute courage, and the hand resting on the shield is unforgettable in its perfection. Ghiberti contributed the *St Matthew*, patron of the money-changers; and later on Andrea Verrocchio presented his *Incredulity of St Thomas*, where the over-elaborate treatment of folds in the bronze togas and the daintily curled head of the apostle point to an intricate and already decadent art style. Last in the line was the Fleming Giambologna with his *St Luke* (1601). Orsanmichele, in fact, summarizes the history of sculpture here, especially with its fine chapel inside containing the famous fourteenth-century tabernacle by Orcagna — slightly overrated, no doubt — and a madonna by Bernardo Daddi (1347).

On the first floor a huge, soberly pillared chamber in the old granary is used for the *Letture di Dante*, an institution of the *trecento* which was revived by Guido Mazzoni about the year 1900. Scholars of widely different backgrounds each expound one canto of the *Divina Commedia* for a keenly interested and attentive audience of ordinary people who are members of the *Società Dantesca*. When they reach the hundredth canto, every few years, they begin again. For this extraordinary poet is one of those rare writers whose work and words disclose new facets and new depths of mystery at every rereading.

An archway joins Orsanmichele to the Palazzo dell' Arte della Lana which underwent a rather glaring restoration in 1905. Like the church, it bears witness to the power of the guilds in the fourteenth century; the wool industry in Florence is said to have given employment to 30,000 workers.

Via Calimala, Via Por Santa Maria and Via Vacchereccia, in that sequence, bring one into the Piazza della Signoria opposite the palace. This route passes the loggia occupied by the Mercato Nuovo, so called to distinguish it from the Mercato Vecchio with its loggia by Vasari; it was demolished at the end of the last century when the city was subjected to drastic alterations by planners who were indifferent to the claims of the past. The new loggia, dating from the mid sixteenth century, is quite unremarkable. A modern statue of *Michele di Lando*, firmly planted in its niche, is the work of a sculptor ingenuous enough to imagine he was creating a symbol of democracy; but today historians have proved that Di Lando was no more than an ambitious upstart. Hidden away at the other end of the loggia is *Il Porcellino*, a great favourite with the common people of Florence. This is a bronze copy by Pietro Tacca of an antique statue of a boar in the Uffizi, a perceptive and forceful study of a wild animal.

> *The great boar in the market-place*
> *This morning fed upon narcissus*

wrote Jean-Louis Vaudoyer; for the market is always full of flowers and the base of Villani's statue is adorned with the pink, white and flame-coloured spears of gladioli.

Clearly visible at the end of the next street is the tall, stern building in which the mediaeval history of Florence was made : the Palazzo Vecchio. At the top is a massive battlemented gallery with Guelph embrasures, and above it soars the tower that symbolized the might of this city : no rival to the inimitable tower in the Campo at Siena, but better proportioned. The space in front of the Palazzo is virtually an open-air museum : the fountain, the statues in bronze and marble all mark important phases in Italian art. The political centre of the city was here. A disc in the pavement indicates the spot where Girolamo Savonarola was burnt on 23 May 1498. Another at the side of the palace commemorates the restoration of freedom on 11 August 1944.

The time to see this piazza is on a holiday. Perhaps when the *Calcio* takes place, and the palace façade in the background is hung with tapestries; or when the trumpeters appear on the balcony wearing the city's device of the red lily on their chests. At night the palace is aglow with the unforgettable *fiaccolata* ; all along the main outlines of this fortress are set thousands of little oil lamps which flame and flicker as the breeze plays round them. A few years ago the same thing used to be done with the dome of St Peter's in Rome. The spectacle is most impressive when the flood-lights are turned off. Not that the normal electric lighting is not

THE COURTYARD OF THE PALAZZO VECCHIO

successful in its way, and even mysterious in its effect; but that steady illumination is outshone by the intense vitality and joyous dancing fires of the *fiaccolata*.

Near the entrance to the palace, filled with the scent of flowers in the month of May, stands the Loggia de' Lanzi, the largest of these galleries in Florence.

This building, dating from 1380, was designed with the audacity of precocious youth. According to Mario Salmi, the three great arches which are the keynote of the monument owe their significance to the three arches of Constantine's Basilica. Originally intended for civic ceremonies and subsequently converted into a guard-house for the German soldiers, known as Lanzi, of the Grand Duke Cosimo, the Loggia is now a showcase for some exquisite pieces of sculpture.

Benvenuto Cellini's *Perseus* and Giambologna's *Rape of the Sabines* are prominently displayed in the arches. If the latter work really amounts to no more than an exercise in virtuosity in which the spiralling composition of over-formal nudes is punctuated by the most

DAVID, BY MICHELANGELO
(DETAIL OF THE ORIGINAL IN THE ACCADEMIA)

deplorably theatrical gestures, there is compensation in the *Perseus*, which is one of those works that are sufficient reason in themselves for a visit to Florence. The powerfully modelled body, from the winged feet to the very ends of the slender fingers holding up the Gorgon's head, is wholly realistic; the jeweller's eye for detail and firm but sensitive technique is apparent in the delicately chased sword-hilt; the almost morbid sophistication

71

of the late Renaissance is evident in the decoration of the pedestal, especially in the relief of *The Rescue of Andromeda*. All these elements, which contrast without clashing, express the complexity and superabundant talents of Cellini, who was indeed typical of the *cinquecento*. Over the truncated corpse of the monster the son of Danae stands erect in the calm certainty of triumph. The head, from which the blood drips in a stream of bronze, has lost its potency : it is the victor who brings one to a halt.

The inner courtyard of the Palazzo Vecchio is also a study in elegant refinement. Narrow, with high, austere walls looming above it, the coolness and the clear murmur of its fountain make this a pleasant retreat, and even more so when summer is at its height. The neo-Pompeian decoration of this *cortile* was adopted at the time of a marriage in 1565 uniting the Habsburg and Medici families. The shafts of the columns are faced with stuccoes which were regilded not long ago : a riot of palm leaves, scrolls, mascarons, beasts — shown face to face in the heraldic style, dumpy cupids, and those heavy swags that the Della Robbia had already made fashionable. A little winged boy carrying a fish stands over the basin in the centre of the *patio:* Verrocchio's successful attempt to reproduce the graceful art of Ancient Greece for Lorenzo de' Medici. It is difficult to believe that the sculptor could have created this enchanting figurine and the cruel-faced statue of Colleoni at Venice within a few months of one another.

Inside the palace are the Sala dei Dugento, whose excellent acoustic properties make it an admirable concert hall, and a number of rooms comprising a museum filled with later works of art which are more instructive than beautiful. Here, Vasari, the great chronicler of Italian art and himself a prolific though not outstanding painter, spared no efforts. His frescoes in the Sala del Cinquecento may well give grounds for regret that those commissioned by the Republic from Michelangelo and Leonardo da Vinci were, through a series of mishaps, never accomplished. The Gonfaloniere had instructed Michelangelo to illustrate the victorious battle against the Pisans at Cascina. The painter, who was living with the dyers in Sant' Onofrio, set to work with his characteristic intensity and passion; when Julius II summoned him to Rome, he simply abandoned his cartoons to the injudicious admiration of his contemporaries, without finishing the task that had been entrusted to him. The other memorial of Florentine victories (the battle of Anghiari against Milan in 1440), was to be interpreted by Da Vinci, but this work too was never completed. All that remained was a sketch, faithfully copied by Rubens at a later date, which does indeed portray the *pazza bestialissima*, the bestial ferocity of the fighting.

The unfinished state of these two frescoes is, moreover, very significant. For the Republic that had ordered them collapsed soon afterwards on the return of the Medici, and Vasari and his pupils have celebrated in paint the easy triumph of these parvenus. In every room throughout the palace there is hardly anything else to see. Due homage is paid to Leo X, Clement VII, Eleanor of Toledo (wife of Cosimo I), Giovanni delle Bande Nere, and as many again. The visitor finds nothing to stir him or keep him in this cold and lifeless maze. The single exception is the *studiolo* of Francesco I de' Medici, a secret room with no external opening, magnificently decorated with panels attributed to Bronzino.

On your way out of the palace, at the top of the entrance steps, look at the *Marzocco*, which is worth examining although it is only a copy of the bronze original now in the Bargello. This figure of a lion supporting a lilied shield personifies the mediaeval Republic. Though it is 400 years since Florence lost its independence, the city is proudly conscious that its defeated enemies were at one time obliged to humble themselves at the feet of this king of beasts. Donatello's *Judith* — the original statue — and a copy of Michelangelo's famous *David* that stands here both stress the theme of victorious liberty, and its bitter savour. Judith, Perseus, David, Hercules — all the heroes of the Bible and of mythology are here. Yet the monogram of Christ gleams over the entrance to the palace, a reminder that the city was dedicated to Him in the sixteenth century; and that, therefore, though Christians are sometimes tempted to pay homage to the superman they should not make an idol of him. Florence offers many such instances of this moderation and balance.

At the corner of the Palazzo Vecchio is a final study in contrast. Against the dull gold façade rears the white marble statue of the huge and awkward *Neptune* by Bartolomeo Ammannati above the monumental fountain completed for the Grand Duke Cosimo in 1571. *Il Biancone* has provoked scores of epigrams and it certainly is ugly; but the bronze figures of satyrs and naiads round the rim are masterly creations, and delightful to see. The whole group hints at the theatrical works of the baroque period, of which Rome in particular has so many.

The equestrian statue of Cosimo I is the meeting-place for Tuscan peasants who come here every Friday at midday to sell their grain. With no other sample, sometimes, than a handful of corn, their negotiations are conducted quietly and peaceably, and everyone retires to some *locanda* in the dark little streets near by to seal the contract with a glass of wine.

The Via de' Gondi emerges almost immediately into the Piazza San Firenze, the site of the theatre in Roman times. A stately palace at the top of some steps is found to be a baroque monastery which has, in fact, been taken over for legal use. Its church, however, was not included in the conversion and is still hallowed by the memory of the Florentine saint Philip Neri, that sanguine apostle of youth at the time of the Counter-Reformation. But our real object in this part of the city is not this mediocre

THE MERCATO NUOVO

church but the Badia and the Bargello.
The delicate little steeple with
its elegant *bifore* and the somewhat
rugged Guelph tower right beside it
are as much a part of the Florence
skyline as the cupola and campanile
of the Duomo and the tower of the
Palazzo Vecchio. With the belfries
of Santa Maria Novella and Santa

'IL PORCELLINO'

74

Croce, the square bulk of Orsanmichele and the little dome of San Lorenzo, they are the salient landmarks soaring above the mass of rose-red roofs when one looks down on Florence from the heights of Fiesole or from the Viale de' Colli.

The palace of the Bargello is an extremely fine example of a mediaeval residence and has been very skilfully restored. At one time the *podestà* lived here, but the palace takes its name from the officer who occupied it at the time of the Medici, a sort of chief of police who converted this fortified mansion into a state prison. Today it houses the superbly presented Museo Nazionale, a valuable group of exhibits which was originally part of the Uffizi treasures, together with private collections of considerable importance such as that bequeathed to the museum by Carrand, a Frenchman. Sculpture, ceramics, jewellery, damascened armour and most of the lesser arts are represented, by specimens of such rare quality that they recreate the very presence of mediaeval or Renaissance Florence.

Here again the visitor is conscious of that gravity which one cannot escape in this city. Only the handsome staircase by Neri di Fioravante and the carved escutcheons on the walls, with their extraordinary crests, relieve the severity of this famous courtyard. For many years a scaffold stood in the middle of it and condemned prisoners were executed here; but this was banished in 1782 by Peter Leopold, an enlightened despot who had read Beccaria.

In a room on the ground floor are displayed works by Michelangelo and his pupils. An almost too true-to-life bust of the master by Daniele da Volterra studies them sourly. *The Drunken Bacchus* dates from 1497, a time when Florence was tottering, her arrogance jolted by the exhausting siege of Pisa. 'It is obvious,' said Vasari, 'that in this figure the artist sought to bring diverse elements into marvellous accord, combining youthful male slenderness with plump feminine curves; and the astounding result proved that in his statues he was superior to any other modern sculptor up to that time.' Bacchus on the point of drunken collapse might well be a symbol of the Republic anxious to forget the dark clouds that were only too visible on the horizon. A marble tondo of the Madonna (1504) shows her teaching the Christ Child to read. Her head is turned sadly away because, as she glanced through the Scriptures, she had a presentiment of her Son's crucifixion and of the sword that would pierce her own heart. Critics have often remarked on the knowledge and technical command with which Michelangelo has accentuated here the contrast between the very detailed and complete portions in relief and the deliberately unfinished background. This became a characteristic feature of his style.

In the gallery at the top of the courtyard staircase the very first object

MERCURY

is Giambologna's graceful *Mercury* which has been popularized by illustrations and has even appeared on stamps. Also noteworthy is a stylized bronze *Peacock* by an unknown Tuscan sculptor of the sixteenth century, a surprisingly decorative work. The finest of Donatello's pieces are found in a huge room on this same floor. They include *St George ; David*, with his peculiar little helmet — perhaps the earliest nude in Tuscan sculpture : Suarès linked him with Shakespeare's Mercury; the very

effective bust of *Niccolò da Uzzano ;* the amazing *Young St John* (though some deny this to be Donatello's work); the *Marzocco ; Eros*, and those gay *putti* in the neo-classical style. The presentation of rare exhibits has been improved and the ivories are now separated from the jewellery and metal-work. Limoges crosiers, Venetian swords, Arab ewers and similar products of sophisticated cultures have found here an ideal setting and atmosphere. The collection of medals, the finest in the world, includes Pisanello's well-known portraits of the

DANAË

76

LOGGIA DE' LANZI : PERSEUS

DONATELLO : ST GEORGE

BARGELLO : THE GALLERY

condottieri, emperors, humanists and noble ladies; but due to the shortage of museum staff it is very rarely on view, and then only to specialists. The Cappella del Podestà has frescoes attributed to Giotto and containing a world-famous portrait of Dante which was, however, rather ineptly restored by an enthusiastic painter of the Romantic period.

Not to be missed on the second floor are Verrocchio's *David* and Cellini's original models for the *Perseus* in the Loggia de' Lanzi, variants of particular interest for their spontaneity. The Della Robbia family, Luca, Andrea and Giovanni, are represented by their delightful glazed bas-reliefs in polychrome terracotta. The earlier and more notable examples (there was a sad decline in the traditions of the *bottega*) vary little in colour: the same celestial blue always paired with white; with just an occasional touch of gold and green in the fruits and foliage of the ornamental garlands. The subject too was generally the same: the Mother of God. Yet monotony is averted by the variety of postures, the charm of the adoring angels and the ingenious selection of emblems. Sometimes Mary is being crowned by the hands of the Creator, sometimes she

BARGELLO : THE DRUNKEN BACCHUS, BY MICHELANGELO

sits enthroned in a garden, the Child leaning toward the roses, sometimes three angels surround them, singing the *Gloria*.

Opposite the Bargello, the Badia Fiorentina, which has been considerably altered throughout the ages, is all that remains of a Benedictine abbey. This was one of the most venerable foundations in Italy, for its patron was Ugo, Margrave of Tuscany, who died in 1006, and it was established during the reign of the Ottos. This prince would be unknown to most people today but for the tomb that Mino da Fiesole designed for him in the Badia in 1480 or thereabouts. Like the unknown subject of a similar portrait in the Museo Nazionale, Ugo might say: '*Ed io da Mino o avuto il lume.*' 'Mino gave me my fame.' Only

BARGELLO : DAVID,
BY VERROCCHIO

BADIA : THE MADONNA APPEARING TO ST BERNARD, BY FILIPPINO LIPPI

the Florentine aristocracy still celebrates his anniversary on 21 December. Some frescoes by Giotto, which Vasari had spoken of, were recently uncover-ed in this church. But the chief and longstanding attraction here is a painting by Filippino Lippi of especial brilliancy — *The Madonna Appear-ing to St Bernard*. How pleasant it is to linger in the quiet church and examine in detail her candid profile. The clamour and bustle of the oldest part of Florence is outside, but all is serenity here, with only an occasional beggar at prayer or asleep in a corner; a reminder that the Paupers' Mass instituted by La Pira is celebrated in this church.

Slowly the shadows of evening fall over Mary's attendant angels and reach the folds of Bernard's ample white robe; and the visitor thinks tranquilly of the innumerable treasures in the vast *gallerie* to be seen on the morrow.

THE BARGELLO AND THE TOWER OF THE BADIA

THE UFFIZI

THE UFFIZI: THE HOLY FAMILY, BY MICHELANGELO (DETAIL)

THE GALLERIES AND MUSEUMS

For an inside view of Florence the tourist must be able to take his time
and his ease. You can spend a pleasant morning simply watching
the round of work and play in the city.

The leisurely progress of the *carrozzelle* — still happily in use — is
a great aid to contemplation. Two or three of them have their permanent
stand close by the Palazzo Vecchio; coachman and horse seem inseparable,
in fact. About ten o'clock in the morning they trot unhurriedly out of
the narrow little Vicolo del Corno, all spruced up. But the best way to go
is on foot. There is plenty of simple enjoyment to be had wandering
around the little shops in the market near San Lorenzo, haggling over a
copy of Boccaccio with the second-hand booksellers who have their open-
air stalls by the porch of the Annunziata, choosing some photographs of

pictures, or engravings, or a few trifling souvenirs below the Uffizi galleries — and never neglecting all the while to look at the people themselves. More substantial pleasures exist for the gourmand; walking, in any case, soon gives one an appetite. Fortunately there's no lack of places where people forgather between eleven and midday to enjoy enticing *petits fours*, delicious anchovy sandwiches or mouth-watering pastries and drink a frothy *cappuccino* or a vermouth. And one sets off again with renewed strength, ready to give all one's attention to that palace façade or this medallion against the pale golden stone which the guide does not mention, or the unknown chapel glimpsed at the end of an alley.

In a relaxed mood after your saunter through the streets, you will be in the right state of mind for the great museums.

The Galleria degli Uffizi and the Palazzo Pitti form

MUSEO ARCHEOLOGICO:
ETRUSCAN WARRIOR'S
STELE

a unit that is perhaps unequalled in the world. Much of the tourist's time will be spent in the dozens of rooms comprising these galleries. However, there is a good deal to be said for beginning with the sources before embarking on the long round that brings one ultimately to the peaks from which one views practically all the highest achievements in European art.

The Museo Archeologico occupies a palace in the Via della Colonna to which are attached some charming and attractively laid-out gardens. The contents of the museum makes it an unrivalled source of information for anyone interested in the Etruscan and the Roman eras in this region. The pleasure and satisfaction to be found in this great museum, with its infinite variety of artistic riches,

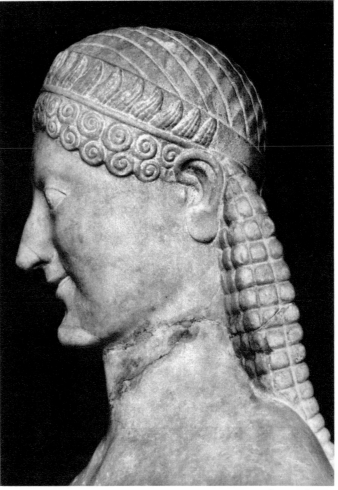

MUSEO ARCHEOLOGICO: THE APOLLO OF ANCONA (DETAIL)

are too often overlooked. First and foremost, it brings to life for us, in a series of small rooms with charts to aid our imagination, that mysterious race who, from Tarquinia to Fiesole, from Volterra to Chiusi, Porsenna's city, have left so many traces of their activity — traces that are all the more precious because we are still not able to decipher the language of these men. The numerous inscriptions on these funeral monuments have the attraction of total mystery for us. Look at the engraved warrior's stele with the longest Etruscan inscription known to us. If the man's likeness had been shown full face it would have automatically called to mind a mediaeval tombstone for the inscription is set round the edge in the same way. In profile, this soldier seems to be still standing and very much alive, with a round shield in his hand and an astonishing crested helmet on his head. What is most striking here, in fact, is the vibrant life that fills the gods on the terracotta pediments taken from temples as much as the human figures seated on their monumental tombs. The smiling men, pointed of nose and chin, and affectionate women, never far from their husbands, are not dead people. Our consciousness of their presence is still more accentuated by the fact that these faces carved in terracotta are most often intact, which is not the case with the majority of antique statues that have survived. An Etruscan museum leaves no room for boredom. However, this is by no means the only collection here; there is almost too much to see without exhaustion.

An excellent display of bronzes is found in the rotunda where the *Idolino* stands and in the gallery leading to it. This is a figure in the style of Praxiteles of a young athlete who is shown offering a libation after his victory in the palaestra; it was found at Pesaro in about 1530, to the great joy of the humanists and the Dukes of Urbino, well-known patrons of the arts. The wonderful discoveries of that century, which had begun with the finding of the 'Laocoon spoken of by Pliny' in the palace of Titus, thrilled an entire people. At this end of the gallery is the notable *Chimaera* from Arezzo, a fifth-century Etruscan bronze in which suffering is realistically conveyed by the unorthodox design. The right leg bears an inscription. A hunt in the section where Greek and Etruscan vases are kept will bring to light the famous *François Vase* which was found

MUSEO ARCHEOLOGICO: THE CHIMAERA OF AREZZO

near Chiusi in 1844, a signed masterpiece of archaic Attic ceramic ware. Zeus in his chariot has the pointed nose and chin that were characteristic of the Etruscans.

The Egyptian rooms close by are of great importance and enable one to make useful comparisons with the Greek and Etruscan civilizations. Also to be found among all these splendours are frescoes and copies of frescoes assembled in reconstructions of interiors from Etruscan necropoles.

However lengthy your visit, it will be of absorbing interest, and you cannot leave the museum without getting one of the keepers to show you the Etruscan tombs which have been brought from their original sites and re-erected in the garden. Take one more look, too, at the *Apollo*, an archaic Greek statue in the entrance hall. This superb work, which came from Ancona, illustrates to

MUSEO ARCHEOLOGICO:
THE IDOLINO

what extent Etruscan art was indebted to Greece while also indicating the subtle differences which marked the genuine originality of Etruria. The silence here is a perfect accompaniment to meditation.

ACCADEMIA: WEDDING CHEST SHOWING THE MARRIAGE OF BOCCACIO ADEMARI
AND LISA RICASOLI (DETAIL)

In the Accademia di Belle Arti one is swamped by tourists once more, for everyone is drawn there by Michelangelo's *David*. Long after leaving Florence, this figure lingers in the memory. One copy, which we have seen, stands in front of the Palazzo Vecchio; another adorns the famous Piazzale Michelangiolo close to San Miniato. The original has been in the Accademia since 1873, displayed in a specially created rotunda suitably lit to set off the statue.

After finishing a *Pietà* for St Peter's, a work of still, controlled sorrow, Michelangelo Buonarroti returned from Rome to Florence in 1501 with the intention, tradition has it, of obtaining a very unusual commission. Since 1481 there had lain in the courtyard of the Opera del Duomo a huge block of marble. Agostino di Duccio had done his best to make something of it but had been obliged to give up his attempt, leaving the half-worked marble in a condition which made it useless to anyone else — or so it was thought. Sansovino and Da Vinci hung back from the challenge. Michelangelo came and staked his all upon this chance. Six months later the *David* emerged. On 25 January 1504 most of the popular artists in the city, Leonardo da Vinci, the aging Perugino, Filippino Lippi and Botticelli, held a meeting to decide upon a suitable site for this perplexing work. It was decreed finally that *David* — as the personification of communal liberty — should be set on the perron of the Palazzo Vecchio, and there he remained for more than 300 years.

Notwithstanding some disproportion, which was due to the extraordinary difficulties the sculptor had to contend with, it is impossible not to admire the latter's knowledge of anatomy. The over-large hands and feet and underdeveloped thighs are right for an adolescent boy — and David was only fifteen. But most notable of all is the freshness of interpretation. No longer is the magnificent 'slinger' shown *after* his victory but just before he takes up the struggle. Hence the air of defiance, the boyish, tight-lipped anger, the furious glance.

All along the broad passage inside the Accademia which leads to this rotunda are placed other works by the same master: the *Pietà di Palestrina*, tragic in its unfinished state, which was brought here soon after 1940, and the famous *Slaves* which were designed for the mausoleum of Pope Julius II. Everyone knows that the thought of this tomb obsessed Michelangelo for a great part of his career and that the grandiose scheme of Julius II came to nothing. Here are a few of the thirty-two statues that were anticipated in the contract of 1513, and even this was modest in comparison with the initial plan. Two of these prisoners are complete; the originals were given by Roberto Strozzi to François I and are now in the possession of the Louvre. The others, which we see here, are roughhewn pieces, massive, impressive, prisoners indeed of the marble which still encloses them on every side.

This same hall in the Accademia is hung with Brussels tapestries dating from the time of Charles V which provide a magnificent description of the Creation. The most surprising touch here is the inventive talent demonstrated by Bernard van Orley in the innumerable animal figures with which he peoples the earthly paradise.

For the rest, this museum consists of ten rooms or so which contain almost exclusively works by Tuscan painters, chiefly those of the fourteenth century. Several of Giotto's disciples are represented: Taddeo Gaddi and his son Agnolo; Bernardo Daddi (a triptych of *The Coronation of the Virgin*); Giovanni da Milano, who had come from Como but worked at Florence; Niccolò Gerini.... We shall have the opportunity to see many of them again at Santa Croce which has a vast series of frescoes. Among the other primitives found in this gallery, those which seem to me to be the most personal are the 'Master of the Maddalena' — almost barbarous in his manner, and Pacino di Buonaguida, whose pictures of saintly archbishops are particularly convincing in their realism.

The Galleria degli Uffizi is on a par with the Louvre, the Prado, the Hermitage and the Kunsthistorisches Museum in Vienna. It occupies the second floor of an enormous palace (begun by Vasari for Cosimo I and finished before the end of the sixteenth century) which takes the form of two elongated wings connected by an overhead passage and extends from the Piazza della Signoria to the *lungarno* here. Architecturally it is majestic enough but cold, with a vast peristyle which someone in the last century thought fit to decorate with twenty-eight statues of Tuscany's most famous sons.

The name 'Uffizi' means 'offices', and in fact these vast premises were originally destined for the administrative and judicial departments under the rule of the Medici. Gradually the grand dukes took over the upper floor to accommodate the antiques for which they had a taste — like the majority of princes in that period. To the marbles and medals and ivories one Medici after another added paintings without number, while the collection was further augmented by substantial family bequests such as that left by Cardinal Leopold in 1675. Later, when this dynasty died out, the last of the family to bear the name, a woman, managed to prevent the removal of these treasures to Vienna, so they were left where they were. The House of Lorraine continued to enlarge the collection and over the last hundred years it has been necessary to clear the overcrowded Uffizi by sorting out some of the exhibits and putting them into ancillary museums like the Bargello.

Today it comprises five completely separate sections, in addition to the superb Cabinet of Prints and Drawings. These are: a remarkable group of antique sculptures; a unique series of 700 *autoritratti* (portraits of painters by themselves); representatives of the Flemish school, with some other foreign artists; examples of various Italian schools, particularly the Venetians; finally, and most important, an incomparable array of works which indicate the entire development of Tuscan painting. In this book we shall concentrate on the first and last in an attempt to give you some idea of the gallery's riches in these categories.

94

THE UFFIZI: NIOBE WITH ONE OF HER DAUGHTERS

THE UFFIZI: THE MEDICI VENUS (DETAIL)

The building itself might have suffered disastrously in the war. In 1944 the mines which exploded only a short distance away shattered the windows, brought down part of the ceilings and made the vaults dangerously insecure; the galleries were a scene of desolation, though luckily their contents had already been removed in a timely moment. The decorated ceilings, strewn with grotesques of a delicate and sinuous design, have been reconstituted; painters working with the patience of mosaicists gathered together all the separate pieces and, with the aid of photographs, restored most of the decoration to its original state.

To retain a clear and orderly impression of what you have seen and wish to remember and to avoid the blankness which results from mere cramming, it is best to make for the most expressive and finest works among the antique statues and the pictures of the Florentine school. Save any spare time to return (as often as you wish) for another look at those which particularly attract you.

Though not so well stocked as the Museo Nazionale Romano, Museo del Vaticano and Museo dei Conservatori in Rome, the classical section of the Uffizi is certainly worthy of note. The statues are displayed along glazed galleries bordering the rooms where the paintings are on show. The galleries are joined at their far end overlooking the Arno, and from this imposing belvedere can be seen, to the north, the outlines of the *cupolone* and the Palazzo Vecchio, and to the south and west the *lungarni* and bridges. At midday, when all the bells are ringing and this balcony is flooded with sunshine, the impression produced is unforgettable.

The best of the antique pieces are in the octagonal Tribuna (east wing) and the Niobe Room (west wing). In the middle of the Tribuna stands the *Medici Venus* — 'one of the greatest joys that Italy can offer,' Burckhardt said. This bashful goddess in translucent amber-coloured marble dates from the third century BC, and it is our good fortune that she has been only very slightly restored. Round about her, take another look at the *Wrestlers*, or the famous *Arrotino*, an exceptionally realistic work, fully deserving of its renown, from the school of Pergamum, and the *Dancing Faun* of which the head and one arm were restored by Michelangelo.

The various elements of *Niobe and Her Children*, brought here from

THE UFFIZI: THE 'ARROTINO'

THE UFFIZI: MADONNA AND CHILD ENTHRONED, BY CIMABUE

THE UFFIZI: MADONNA AND CHILD ENTHRONED, BY GIOTTO

THE UFFIZI: ADORATION OF THE MA

the Villa Medici in Rome, have been given a room of their own at the other end of the museum. This magnificent group, which may have been derived from marble originals of the school of Praxiteles, was discovered in 1588 in the course of excavations near the Lateran. The theme is a myth which was immortalized by Ovid: the anger of Diana transfixing, one after the other, the children of this granddaughter of Zeus who had dared to challenge the goddess. All are shown struck down and overwhelmed in an impressive diversity of poses. This son is already dead; that daughter is drawing her last breath in the arms of a brother. But the climax of emotion is reached in the figure of the mother as she tries to save the youngest girl at least; in her distraught face turned up to heaven are defiance, outrage, despair....

But having paid our due respects to the few reflections of Athens or Pergamum which illumine the Uffizi, it is with real pleasure that we shall bask in the springtime radiance that emanates from the Tuscan painters.

Some radical transformations in the arrange-

THE UFFIZI: ANNUNCIATION, BY SIMONE MARTINI AND LIPPO MEMMI (DETAIL)

ment of the museum have been carried out since the war and more recently still : the internal architecture of the rooms, the lighting, the positioning of the exhibits — almost everything has been modified. The notice *Sistemazione Provvisoria* occasionally seen on a wall means in effect that the system here is experimental and may be drastically altered in a few weeks. So there is room to hope that some errors in the general layout, which has clearly been modernized and in some instances improved, will be rectified in time.

The first impression is good. For the first time in the Uffizi the two great *Madonnas* by Cimabue and Giotto are really seen at their best under a natural light in a white-walled room that has been made very high, with the timber-work left visible. Thirty years separate these two pictures which were executed respectively for the churches of Ognissanti and Santa Trinità; yet they suggest a much greater division in time. One perceives here what genius Giotto showed in his innovations, and Santa Croce will confirm this view.

The intuitive American critic Berenson had this to say: 'In the Cimabue we patiently decipher the lines and colours, and we conclude at last that they were intended to represent a woman seated, men and angels standing by or kneeling. To recognize these representations we have had to make many times the effort that the actual objects would have required, and in consequence our feeling of capacity has not only not been confirmed, but actually put in question. With what sense of relief, of rapidly rising vitality, we turn to the Giotto ! Our eyes have scarcely had time to light on it before we realize it completely — the throne occupying a real space, the Virgin satisfactorily seated upon it, the angels grouped in rows about it. Our tactile imagination is put to play immediately.... Giotto contrives to render, out of all the possible outlines, out of all the possible variations of light and shade that a given figure may have, only those that we must isolate for special attention when we are actually realizing it.... Nothing here but has its architectonic reason.'

Giotto led the way, and following in his steps soon after came most of the great artists of a surprisingly early Renaissance.

A low-ceilinged room near by is devoted to the charming painters of the Sienese school, though it is disappointing to see Simone Martini's *Annunciation* in such poor lighting as this. Martini is known for his work on the papal palace, but this picture is his masterpiece despite the fact that it was finished by Lippo Memmi. Against a gleaming gold background the celestial messenger humbly kneels, his diapered wings contrasting strangely with the travelling cloak — rather like a Scottish plaid — that floats from his shoulders. The golden letters of his salutation dissolve into the background of the reredos. Mary herself is seated on a marble throne decorated with Cosmati work which immediately calls to mind some of those old Roman churches that won the praise of Emile Mâle.

Her posture is faultless in its delicacy: no other artist, perhaps, has managed so well to suggest at one and the same time the anxious modesty, utter humility, radiant saintliness and noble birth of the Virgin. Above these two figures flashing seraphim surround the Holy Ghost hovering in the atmosphere.

Less significant are the works of Simone's successors and of the Florentine disciples of Giotto assembled here at the Uffizi. Among these are paintings by Ambrogio and Pietro Lorenzetti, and Taddeo Gaddi, polyptychs by Daddi and one of the very few painted panels by the sculptor Orcagna still in existence. The development of the Renaissance seemed keyed to the increasing potentialities of the Tuscan painters, culminating in that universal being, Leonardo da Vinci. As early as the fourteenth century this school evinced a spiritual exaltation and an intellectual hunger.

The two *Adorations of the Magi* by Lorenzo Monaco and Gentile da Fabriano are both characterized by an appealing and sophisticated orientalism. These panels are in fact an introduction to that completely different world of the *quattrocento*, with all its variety and richness. A world that is typified by the systematic extremes of Paolo Uccello (see his *Battle of San Romano* in the next room) — geometrical preoccupations, contempt for primary colours.... But novelty is not always genius.

The first genius was Masaccio who has hardly anything here apart from a picture which he and Masolino worked on together: *The Madonna and St Anne* — an exceedingly instructive and well-presented work. Note the combinations of red and yellow and red and pink in the angels' robes. For the time being, at any rate, Lippi's pictures are still kept together. Fra Filippo was of mean parentage and had been brought up by the Carmelites, entering their order at the age of fifteen. But the corruption and laxity of life in Florence soon had their effect on him, and he eventually abducted from her convent at Prato a young nun who had posed for his studies of the Virgin; she bore a son, Filippino, who also became a painter. There is an obvious similarity between all Filippo's different pictures of the Madonna and the Christ Child which leads one to see them as portraits of Filippino and Lucrezia Buti.

Was Filippo a genius? He had an unerring talent and a delicate style; his treatment of landscape was strange and prophetic, and his portraits were cruelly lifelike — the well-known profile of the Duke of Urbino is displayed on an easel in prominent view. But his religious inspiration was limited. Critics have even gone so far as to say that he killed mysticism. In other and simpler words, his Virgin is too worldly, his Christ Child too realistic. Fra Angelico, his senior by twenty years, had never ceased to be conscious of Paradise and adopted it as his natural element. Lippi, to whom Pius II showed extreme indulgence, was a living instance of the break between the asceticism of the middle ages and the sensuality

THE UFFIZI: ADORATION OF THE CHILD, BY FILIPPO LIPPI (DETAIL)

THE UFFIZI: BIRTH OF VENUS, BY BOTTICELLI (DETAIL)

of the Renaissance humanists. It is nonetheless characteristic of Tuscan art that voluptuous pleasure is tempered by intelligence.

With Sandro Botticelli the climax of the next generation of painters is reached. Of all those in the Uffizi he is represented by the most complete cycle of works. The amiable and melancholy Sandro was unusually complex. Like Fra Filippo, he was very much a man of his century — though a more versatile one. With his combination of sentiment and vigour, he veered — according to the ebb and

THE UFFIZI: MADONNA WITH THE POMEGRANATE, BY BOTTICELLI (DETAIL)

flow of reaction to Savonarola — between the mildness of Hellenism and the habit of meditation resulting from an intense devotion to the Virgin in conjunction with a penitential spirit.

At the age of thirty he was in the service of the Medici, living in that pagan wonder that was stimulated in artists by the gardens of San Marco which Lorenzo the Magnificent had lovingly stocked with antique marbles. Besides the cynics out for amusement there were, in this neo-Platonic atmosphere, more serious men who were obsessed with the worthy desire to reconcile the Christian and Hellenic traditions. However

dangerous these Florentine experiments may have appeared for Christian dogma they brought a corresponding influence to bear on Greek mythology : those legends so well known to the humanists of the time were transfigured by the process.

Botticelli's greatest works have been brought or rather crammed together into a small and overcrowded room. Of them all *Venus* suffers least from the wan light overhead; but no situation could detract from the greatness of this

picture of *The Birth of Venus* (1486) of which Politian wrote:

A maiden of unearthly beauty
Urged by the eager Zephyrs
to the shore....

By the calm shores of Cyprus, on a green sea hardly marked by a ripple, the Anadyomene stands radiant in her nakedness while the Zephyrs shower roses upon her, so light a goddess that the great shell barely rocks beneath her weight. As Miomandre charmingly put it: 'She was at the same time inert and heavy with all the secrets of life, and light as down floating in the air.' An exquisite modesty informs her gestures. To the right, Spring is hastening to meet her, carrying a rose-pink cloak scattered with tiny flowers — reassuring protection to the fastidious soul within that perfect body. By the purity of her expression, despite the quivering nostrils, by the elegant refinement of her sloping shoulders and graceful neck, Botticelli has all but ceased to make Venus the incarnation of desire. She has become an idealized vision expressing the syncretism of the Tuscans.

Take a look too at the pictures of Mary near by: the *Madonna with the Pomegranate*, in particular — an even sadder figure showing the characteristic treatment of the neck; and the *Madonna of the Magnificat* who has exactly the same streaming blonde hair and looks like a Christian version of Minerva. These two and the portrayal of Truth in *Calumny* have an undeniable family resemblance to Venus.

The *Primavera* is completely typical of the Florentine Renaissance in its highly intellectual conception; unfortunately the poor lighting makes the orange grove seem even darker than it is. This picture is in fact a transposition of the *Forest of Love*, written by Lorenzo himself, and certain passages by Leon Battista Alberti. Here is what Nello Tarchiani said about it: 'In this mysterious composition which may have been based on advice from Politian and some lines by Horace and Lucretius, Sandro shows Chloris with Zephyr in pursuit behind and Flora before her, while *Venus Genetrix* looks on benevolently. Blindfold Love shoots his arrow he knows not where, the Graces perform their leisurely dance, and with his wand Mercury drives away the clouds from the leafy trees with their golden fruit. Where are we, and what are all those divine beings doing there? Dozens of interpretations have been put forward, but the problem remains insoluble. Perhaps it is an oblique account of an event in the lives of the Medici which has so far escaped notice. Some development seems about to take place: everyone appears to be waiting for something extraordinary but indefinable. Despite the general air of serenity, the very atmosphere thrills with anxious impatience. Not all the clouds have been chased away yet by the wand of the celestial messenger.'

The mystery surrounding this artist will never be entirely dispelled because his most voluptuous works are lost to us; caught up in the wave of asceticism unleashed by Savonarola, Botticelli burned these in 1490 or thereabouts. However, the *Minerva*, which was very well restored recently and is now placed in a corner of this same room, plainly suggests, beneath its greeny-blue sky, the apotheosis of the peace that Lorenzo de' Medici sought.

The full range of Tuscan art in the Uffizi is not limited to one line of development, as witness such splendid offshoots as Piero della Francesca, Albertinelli, Lorenzo di Credi and other more eminent masters of painting.

Leonardo da Vinci's *Annunciation* is extremely well presented — by itself, and lit from the side. This is a youthful work in which the background landscape hints at the artist's early difficulties in handling space. Slightly later in date (after 1481) is the strange *Adoration of the Magi*, a sketch on a wooden panel which never progressed beyond the first stage

THE UFFIZI: PRIMAVERA,

of brownish colour, with faces and hands barely discernible. The theory is that, while working on this study which was to synthesize all his researches, Da Vinci stopped abruptly because he had found his way — a way that led him far from the traditional retinue with its clutter of figures which was his commission. The impalpable gradations of light are a signpost to future masterpieces. But except in his drawings Leonardo never again created such moving figures as in this group to the left of the Child, conveying at once the suffering of the poor as they awaited the Messiah and the birth of their hope.

Michelangelo's *Holy Family* (the 'Doni' tondo) is memorable for other reasons. This picture too diverges from the traditions of the Tuscan school; but in this case the painter has the eye of a sculptor and is chiefly concerned with the relation of bodies to the space around them. His forms are not static — on the contrary. Notice the bending motion of the adoring Madonna as she leans back to take her Son — not to hold Him out to Joseph, as Vasari maintained; see how the Child, slipping, grabs hold of His Mother's hair — a typical gesture in young children; watch St Joseph endeavouring to cope with this burden. The triple movement suggests a pyramid inscribed within a circle. Also out of the ordinary are the strident, clashing colours : pink with a dash of yellow, strong orange and beige, cerulean blue. The artist knew that with the use of these almost metallic tints, which reflect light without absorbing any of it, he would be able to give dimension to his shapes. The naked and indifferent youths who lurk unaccountably in the background (as in one of Signorelli's *Madonnas*) might be taken as symbolizing the pagan world.

The final pages of the story of Tuscan painting at the Uffizi bring us to the *cinquecento* and more than one artist of rare talent. Andrea del Sarto, 'the faultless Andrea', was fascinated by the possibilities of chiaroscuro. Bronzino produced several court portraits showing off the beautiful fabrics made in Florence. Two extraordinary works by Pontormo decorate the Tribuna from the Villa Medici; another notable picture by this engaging painter is *The Disciples at Emmaus* in which the whole gamut of orange shades is used to astonishing effect in the disciples' robes.

The Tuscan school really had its golden age in the fifteenth century. The climax of Hellenic sculpture 2000 years earlier extended over little more than two generations; such a luxuriant flowering can be nothing else than exceptional. Fortunate indeed are we today who can in this same spot taste of that divine spring from which the Florentines drew their inspiration.

Of course no visitor will leave the Uffizi without having at least glanced at the magnificent works by other Italian artists, from Correggio to the Venetians, which cannot be discussed in detail here. It is worth noting that the Raphael collection has been augmented by the *Leo X* which used to be in the Pitti. Shown between two of his intimates, this

THE UFFIZI: MADONNA OF THE MAGNIFICAT, BY BOTTICELLI

son of Lorenzo is painted with a cruel clarity and not the least suggestion of flattery. The canvas had been brought to the studio here for restoration and stayed on this side of the Arno. Such was the case also with Titian's *Flora*, which will always appeal to youthful visitors from Northern Europe when they come to Tuscany for the first time, and the beautiful nudes derived from his *Venus* at Dresden.

In the western gallery a few steps used to lead into a long series of corridors which were built in 1565 to connect the Uffizi with the Pitti,

passing over the Ponte Vecchio. Today these are shut off, for the restoration of this passage is linked with that of the Ponte Vecchio and its approaches.

The Galleria Palatina, on the first floor of the Palazzo Pitti, seems much like a continuation of the Uffizi; except that here more space is given to the schools of Umbria, Bologna, Naples, Venice and Rome, and to the Flemish and Spanish artists. The setting above all is totally different. At the Pitti an attempt seems to have been made to reconcile the majestic works of great masters with the sumptuous ornament of princely apartments. Everywhere you see ceilings richly decorated with

frescoes and stuccoes, porphyry vases and superb Gobelins tapestries, alabaster tables and imposing furniture. As at Fontainebleau, Compiègne, and Versailles, you are confronted by magnificence — that of the grand-ducal period.

Saturn, Jupiter, Mars, Apollo and Venus adorn the first rooms of the long façade. Pietro da Cortona covered the high ceilings with frescoes depicting the glory of Cosimo I — luminous, airy painting which takes its place among the finest examples of this art genre in which the Romans of the seventeenth century excelled. Nowadays people are but little impressed by these flying draperies and this mythological jumble: *Minerva*

Snatching the Young Cosimo from Venus to Take Him to Hercules; Cosimo, Led by Fortune and Hercules, Receives from Jupiter the Crown of Immortality, and so on. These ceilings in the Pitti, together with those in the Palazzo Barberini in Rome, mark a date in international art. Other painted ceilings in the Galleria Palatina are of less interest. Some of the pictures displayed in the rooms are much move worthy of attention.

First and foremost, the works of Raphael, dazzling in their beauty. The *Madonna del Granduca* was so called because Fernando II, who had bought it in 1799, could not bear to be separated from it and took it

THE UFFIZI: FLORA, BY TITIAN (DETAIL)

THE UFFIZI: MADONNA WITH THE GOLDFINCH, BY RAPHAEL (DETAIL)

everywhere. It was one of the earliest (about 1506) of Sanzio's series of forty-two madonnas — the very pattern of purity, youth and what the Italians call *signorilità*.

Bernard Berenson puts it thus: 'Sanzio produced a type, the composite of Ferrarese, Central Italian, and Florentine conceptions of female beauty, which, as no other, has struck the happy mean between the

THE UFFIZI: POPE LEO X, BY RAPHAEL

PALAZZO PITTI: MADONNA DELLA SEGGIOLA, BY RAPHAEL

instinctive demands of life and the more conscious requirements of art.'

The *Madonna della Seggiola* is too well known, perhaps, through the reproductions beyond number and of very unequal quality which have made it universally current. But this beautiful Roman girl from the Traste-vere is extremely attractive even if less ideally perfect than other madonnas. Some of these lovely women have a hint of mystery in their faces. It is surely impossible not to respond to the deep glance of the *Donna Velata* (portrait of La Fornarina, the artist's favourite model who, according to Morelli, also inspired his *San Sisto Madonna* at Dresden). Behind the less

PALAZZO PITTI: DONNA VELATA, BY RAPHAEL

gracious beauty of *Maddalena Doni* stretches a landscape in the style of Perugino, a feature which is repeated in *Angelo Doni*. The clarity and precision of the drawing in both these portraits relate them to fifteenth-century art and to that of Umbria in particular.

The Uffizi and the Pitti together contain such an abundance of Titian's works that it is possible to gain a complete knowledge of this artist in Florence. The *Maddalena*, work of his maturity (1531), had been commissioned by Federigo da Gonzaga who wanted it to be 'as beautiful and as unhappy as possible'. This voluptuous allegory is the exact antithesis of Donatelli's inspiration — the sculptural forms are barely concealed beneath the streaming fair hair, with golden highlights here and there. In similar style is the *Bella* dressed in heavy brocade, the probable model for the *Urbino Venus*.

Since the advent of Proust most people are especially drawn to works which show insight into male psychology; two masculine portraits which are the pride of the Pitti will therefore claim careful attention. Titian produced his picture of the notorious *Pietro Aretino* in 1548, when he was seventy-two — too old to humour his models any longer: perhaps the word should be 'victims'. This *is* the poet who paraded the vices he practised and others he did not... his imperious glance, his triumphant fatuity, his gigantic body gaudily decked in silk and velvet finery. With justification it has been described as 'one of the greatest examples of the art of catching character unawares'. The *Portrait of a Gentleman* with a gold chain round his neck clearly betrays the influence of Giorgione. The light of battle shines in his sharp blue-green eyes, while his face has been fragmented into areas of shadow producing forceful contrasts. Thoughtful visitors should also go and see Tintoretto's *Luigi Cornaro*, startlingly life-like with his scanty beard and that look of candour and sadness that some old men have.

Fra Bartolomeo brings us back to Florence. He was already an artist of renown at the time of his conversion by Savonarola, and after he became a Dominican friar he painted nothing but religious pictures. The *Descent from the Cross* is a masterpiece in its colouring and emotional content. His pupil Andrea del Sarto — much in evidence in the

PALAZZO PITTI:
PORTRAIT OF
ANGELO DONI,
BY RAPHAEL

church of the Annunziata — is represented in the Pitti by an *Annunciation* that is very characteristic of his master's style and a *St John the Baptist as a Child*, which is bolder and more vigorous, combining grace with grandeur.

This grace was the mark of a certain mannerism and left its stamp on Perugino's models, whose faces usually stand out against radiant landscapes suffused with light. The most notable of his works here are the *Descent from the Cross* and the *Maddalena*, very young and essentially pure, with her amber-skinned oval face. Perugino was the only Italian painter to have won the notice and praise of the French at the end of the fifteenth century.

Nowadays their vote would probably go to *The Concert*, beyond doubt a great work whether by Giorgione or by Titian, as some modern

PALAZZO PITTI: VIRGIN IN ADORATION, BY PERUGINO (DETAIL)

PALAZZO PITTI: ST JOHN THE BAPTIST, BY ANDREA DEL SARTO (DETAIL)

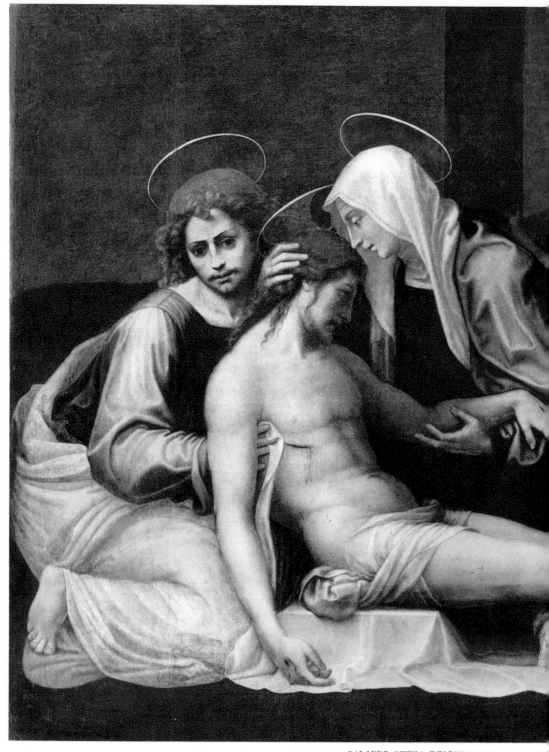

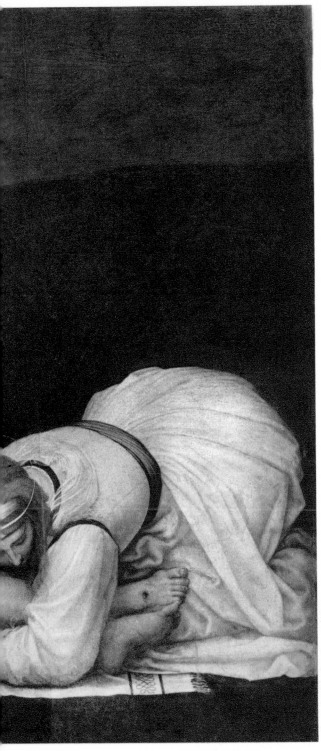

critics claim. One's gaze is riveted by this cleric's face which conveys with a suggestion of sorrow the very essence of the music.

To end the visit, those who wish to exhaust the curiosities that may be seen can wander about the royal apartments with their eighteenth- and nineteenth-century decoration, coming across a Titian here, a Sodoma there — which is bound to be a portrait of St Sebastian.

In springtime, the great season in Florence, the Pitti has its oases of quiet. One of these is the Gallery of Modern Art which, if it has no work of real genius to offer, possesses others that show an excellent sense of colour and a genuine understanding of the Tuscan countryside. Another is the Museo degli Argenti with its collection of jewellery and goldsmiths' work — provided it opens on the same days as the Gallery.

Now is a good opportunity to seek out those agreeable little museums where the masterpieces give no less pleasure for being few and far between and are more accessible. There are enough to suit

A BARTOLOMEO

CENACOLO DI SANT' APOLLONIA: LAST SUPPER, BY ANDREA DEL CASTAGNO

every taste scattered throughout the city. Take the Museo Bardini, on the left bank, which is a pendant to the Bargello — for sculpture and carpets in particular — and shamefully neglected by tourists. Generally speaking, the only drawback is in the infrequent hours, or even days, of

admittance. It is necessary to find out exactly what these are. Keeping to the right bank of the Arno, the mediaeval Palazzo Davanzati situated near the Central Post Office has some pleasing murals illustrating an Italian version of the *Chastelaine de Vergy*, furnishings and fittings of the Florentine house between the fifteenth and

seventeenth
centuries, and a
museum of
handicrafts.

Some original
drawings by
Michelangelo,
with notes in
his own writing,
and youthful
works like the
*Madonna della
Scala* and the
*Battle of the Cen-
taurs* are among
the exhibits
permanently on
show in the Casa
Buonarroti. To
visit the rest of the mansion, however, would be a waste of time.

At the end of a sightseeing day in Florence you could not do better
than go for rest and contemplation to one of the *cenacoli*. These are the
refectories of former monasteries in which an artist, often a very great
one indeed, has depicted the Last Supper of Christ on the end wall.

SUPPER, BY ANDREA DEL SARTO

PALAZZO PITTI: CONCERT, BY GIORGIONE (OR TITIAN)

There are several of these Last Suppers in Florence. One by Orcagna, probably among the oldest, is or rather used to be in the *cenacolo* of Santo Spirito, on the left bank. There is practically no trace of it now, but the refectory itself contains wonderful fragments of some very ancient Romanesque sculptures and an *Angel* by Tino da Camaino which is one of the finest he ever did. Ognissanti has a well-preserved *cenacolo*, with a fresco by Domenico Ghirlandaio (he repeated it later in the convent of San Marco) which just antedates that other famous *Last Supper* by Leonardo da Vinci at Milan. At Ognissanti the figures are rather badly arranged but to compensate for this the wall of the chamber seems to open out on to an exquisite landscape scattered with birds in flight. It is a landscape again that lends charm to the anonymous *cenacolo da Foligno*, to be found in the Via Faenza. This work combining the styles of Umbria and Tuscany may be by Perugino. In it depth is created by means of a forest of magnificent pillars of antique type which vary in volume according to their position in the perspective. The *Last Supper* in the old convent of Sant' Apollonia, not far from San Marco, has an architectural quality. Forty years before Domenico Ghirlandaio, Andrea del Castagno, its creator, made his seated figures like statues rather than paintings. Andrea, who died young, was also responsible for those famous pictures on view here that were executed for the Villa Pandolfini towards the middle of the fifteenth century; boldly using colour to give the effect of modelling, he has made these figures seem eager to jump out of their frames.

We might go on still further, crossing the Florence-Arezzo railway line to reach the old abbey of San Salvi which contains Andrea del Sarto's masterpiece, begun in 1519 : a *Last Supper* that is airy and spacious yet lacking in emotional appeal. But one must know when to call a halt and put off until the next day — in order to look with fresh eyes upon the world of faith, fervour and action — delights which the painters of the mendicant orders have left at Santa Croce, Santa Maria Novella and San Marco.

PALAZZO PITTI : PORTRAIT OF A GENTLEMAN, BY TITIAN (DETAIL)

SANTA MARIA NOVELLA: THE CHIOSTRO VERDE

FAÇADE OF SANTA MARIA NOVELLA

CHURCHES AND PALACES

ANYONE who has studied the layout of the city, from the top of the Campanile, for instance, will be aware of the importance of Santa Croce.

At the beginning of the thirteenth century, when the Minorite friars were becoming more and more active, there was a marshy area between

INSIDE SANTA CROCE

the Arno and a lesser branch. There the humble mendicants settled, at the gates of the crowded city, just as they were doing everywhere else; and the fame and admirable qualities of these monks won them the goodwill of the governing classes. Work on their church of Santa Croce began in 1295 and was resumed in the middle of the next century, the final date of the consecration being 1443. It is, therefore, as old as the Duomo. The largest Franciscan church in the world, Santa Croce still belongs to that order, whose members hold in great reverence a fragment of the True Cross kept here and celebrate with special solemnity the feast of 14 September. The old church has become a patriotic temple, much like the Panthéon in Paris, and plays a prominent role in Florentine life.

In Stendhal's time the earlier and unsatisfactory façade of brick or *rozza*, as it is called here, was still in place. The present-day front, much criticized now and dating, like the campanile, from 1863-1865, was made possible by a munificent gift from an Englishman, Sloane, and the public subscriptions that followed. It is sober and acceptable, and that's all. It seems a pity, though, that this city's wonderful palaces are not matched in quality by the church fronts.

The division into three aisles of the spacious and typically Italian interior of the basilica is all but nominal. As befits the disciples of poverty, the arrangement is austere and bare of all ornament : even the timber-work

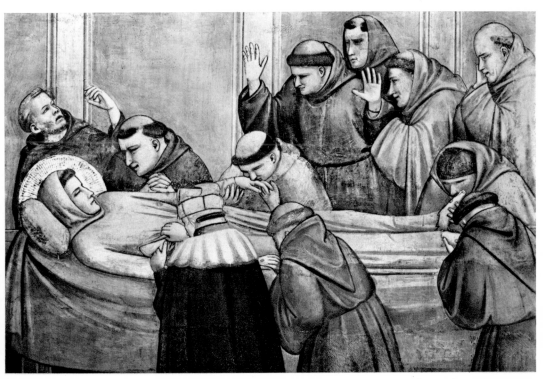

SANTA CROCE: DEATH OF ST FRANCIS OF ASSISI, BY GIOTTO (DETAIL)

in the roof has been left visible. The apse is lit by very tall windows, and chapels of considerable size open on to the wide transepts. In addition, however, to being an agreeable and well-proportioned church conducive to meditation and prayer, Santa Croce is a cemetery containing some 300 tombstones, and virtually a museum of the art of fresco.

Artistically, Santa Croce provides a wealth of conflicting impressions, from Giotto's frescoes to the tomb of Alfieri with the statue of the Countess of Albany by Canova: following the dictates of that age of 'sensibility', he has depicted her weeping for her dead lover. From Donatello's relief in *pietra serena* of the *Annunciation*, close by the very pleasing tomb of Leonardo Bruni, to the modern stained-glass windows that were dedicated to the dead of the first world war. From the mausoleum of Michelangelo by Vasari to the huge frescoes by Agnolo and Taddeo Gaddi. Sightseers are often disconcerted by the number and diversity of things to see. Those who are interested in the primitives should concentrate on the Bardi and Peruzzi chapels (Giotto) and the Castellani and Baroncelli chapels (school of Giotto), all leading off the south transept.

The first two of these bear the names of their patrons who were the most powerful bankers of the first half of the *trecento*. The Peruzzi chapel contains scenes from the lives of St John the Baptist and St John the Evangelist (after 1320), while the Bardi chapel, nearest the choir, portrays the life of St Francis of Assisi (after 1317). These frescoes are among the greatest achievements of the man who was the founder of Tuscan art, ranking with those at Padua and Assisi. The men of the *settecento*, indifferent to these paintings, overlaid them with a thick coat of plaster which was not removed until 1852. Repainted and 'finished' here and there about the year 1860, intelligent restoration has now brought them back to their original state. The backgrounds, which had become almost black, are bright and ethereal once more. Night has given place to day around the pale face of St Clare. In the *Death of St Francis of Assisi*, the most celebrated of these frescoes, the translucent light and the delicate tones touched with pink and pale green are a real discovery. It is easier to recognize the maturity of an art which was destined to win universal acclaim. In *The Raising of Drusiana by St John*, showing the widely

SANTA CROCE: PAZZI CHAPEL

different reactions of a crowd of people, and also in *The Ordeal by Fire Before the Sultan* (in the Bardi chapel) the postures are correct, the action vigorous, and the dramatic setting superb. 'What is lacking in my art was never in nature,' says the epitaph that Politian wrote for the artist in the fifteenth century.

But this restoration was not done without some sacrifice. Parts are missing from the frescoes, sometimes complete figures, which spoils the general effect of the iconographic scheme as it had been designed in the fourteenth century. Hence the disappearance of *St Louis*, *King of France* from the basilica. This can be found in a room close to the sacristy where all the parts that were restored in the last century are on display. It may well have been the first of the very few portraits of this saint existing in Italy : Giotto had painted the now vanished original twenty years after the canonization of this sovereign. The king held the Franciscan girdle in his hand, which implies that from 1320 he was venerated as their protector by the Tertiaries of that order.

On the other side of the south transept is the light and spacious chapel of the Blessed Sacrament with its blend of various elements left by the late *trecento*. The scenes from the life of St Nicholas and even the *Martyrdom of St Apollonia* give considerable pleasure. The Gaddi were already swerving from the course set by their master. Such features as the almond-shaped eyes, recalling Sienese art, the sensuous treatment of the women's heads (probably due to the influence

SANTA CROCE: SCENES FROM THE LIFE OF ST NICHOLAS, BY AGNOLO GADDI, IN THE CASTELLANI CHAPEL (DETAIL)

PIAZZA DELLA SANTISSIMA ANNUNZIATA: FOUNTAIN BY TACCA AND PORTICO
OF THE SERVITE ORDER

of Giovanni da Milano) and similar characteristics noticed here add an agreeably ornate quality to Giottesque art even if they detract from its inestimable majesty. However, Giotto's vigour is still to be seen in the *Miracles of St Sylvester* by Maso di Banco at the other end of the north transept.

SPEDALE DEGLI INNOCENTI: ADORATION OF THE MAGI, BY GHIRLANDAIO (DETAIL)

Try at all costs to find time to see the choir, with its fresco of the *Legend of the Cross* by Agnolo Gaddi, on some ceremonial occasion in the evening. It will be impossible to see the painting in detail, but the powerful lighting enhances the total effect of the interior: the sweep of the apse, the altar with its polyptych and, up above, the great painted crucifix from the school of Giotto.

At the entrance to the cloister is the Museo dell' Opera di Santa Croce; recently renovated, it is now in the process of expansion. Cimabue's *Crucifix* has been restored to its place here, and works by Orcagna and Taddeo Gaddi are also on show. Another item is Donatello's *St Louis of Toulouse*.

Give yourself plenty of time to devote to one of the jewels of Florence, the Pazzi chapel (found at the far end of the cloister) which was begun by Brunelleschi in 1430. The architectural decoration of the interior, with its Corinthian pilasters, is based on the contrast of white with grey, involving the use of *pietra serena*. The pictorial relief (medallions by Luca della Robbia) is very sober; the tiny cupola is painted, in the fashion of the time, to represent the progress of the planets through the sky. There are few creations so fundamentally representative of the Renaissance and showing such a complete grasp of that knowledge of proportion which distinguished Vitruvius and, later on, Palladio. It has the clarity and harmony of the Erechtheion or one of Bach's fugues. 'With all its imperfections, I would not exchange it for the Temple at Ephesus,' admitted Président de Brosses.

The Via Verdi and the Borgo Pinti are working-class streets, grim and narrow and typical of this old quarter of the city. Along them one notices the windows guarded by immense grilles — *inferriate* — and the high walls shadowed by the overhanging eaves of the roofs — *tettoie*. Contemporary civilization seems far away. Yet this rather unimpressive route leads to the church that is undoubtedly held in greatest affection by all sections of the populace: the basilica of the Santissima Annunziata. On the way, stop to look at a small church set inconspicuously at the far end of a courtyard, Santa Maria Maddalena de' Pazzi. Built by Giuliano da San Gallo at the end of the fifteenth century, it was extensively repaired

FRA ANGELICO: ST PETER MARTYR

BUST OF ST ANTONINUS

SAN MARCO: CRUCIFI

FRA ANGELICO

ST DOMINIC

in the seventeenth, although the graceful porch was left untouched. It was dedicated to one of that group of saints in which Florence can take pride; when this humble Carmelite nun died on 25 May 1607 at the age of thirty-eight, the people heaped such masses of roses on her bier that she became known as the 'saint of the flowers'. Santa Maria Maddalena serves as parish church for the French residents in Florence who meet here to celebrate their own special feast days, such as that of St Joan of Arc. A community of Augustines officiates.

The church of the Santissima Annunziata looks out on to a vast and symmetrical square. Prancing in the middle of it is an equestrian statue of the Grand Duke Fernando I by Giambologna, which was cast from bronze cannon seized from the Barbary States at Bona. Happily, this piece of pomposity is counterbalanced by two original fountains. The grand dukes were without exception more than generous to the Annunziata which has in consequence undergone so many transformations that nothing remains of the church erected in the middle of the thirteenth century by the seven saintly founders of the Servite Order. It is fronted by a covered cloister whose walls are decorated with frescoes, unfortunately in very poor condition, by Rosso,

ST FRANCIS OF ASSISI

SAN MARCO: ANNUNCIATION, BY FRA ANGELICO (DETAIL)

SAN MARCO: CORONATION OF THE VIRGIN, BY FRA ANGELICO

Pontormo and, in particular, Andrea del Sarto. The interior of the basilica, strikingly rich in effect with its hundreds of votive lamps, brocade hangings, gilt-coffered ceiling and use of different marbles, is certainly one of the most glittering examples of baroque architecture in Florence. In addition, it is one of the churches in Italy where the most wonderful orchestral performances of sacred music can be heard (perhaps during a ceremonious and long-winded mass), for this theatrical practice still flourishes south of the Alps. Immediately to the left of the entrance is the fifteenth-century marble chapel specially built to house the miraculous

SAN MARCO: DESCENT INTO LIMBO, BY FRA ANGELICO

portrait of a Madonna which was claimed to have been painted by an angel. As is the custom in other parts of Italy too, the fresco is exposed only on certain feast days; for most of the time it is concealed by a massive silver shrine studded with diamonds. All day there is a constant stream of worshippers at this altar, and young brides like to leave an offering of flowers there.

The Spedale degli Innocenti occupies another side of the square — one of the earliest foundling hospitals in Europe. To draw attention to the charitable enterprise that functioned there and touch the hearts and pockets of passers-by, it was decided to decorate the façade with figures of babies. This task was entrusted to a sculptor of genius, Andrea della Robbia, and his medallions in majolica with their blue backgrounds are so lifelike that they always evoke a response.

The convent of San Marco, on the piazza of the same name is, without doubt, the most famous Dominican

FRA ANGELICO: MADONNA AND CHILD (DETAIL)

foundation in the world. The first sight of it awakens a subdued delight in visitors drawn here by thoughts of Fra Angelico. Also associated with this monastery are three other preaching friars who lived within

SAN MARCO: DESCENT FROM THE CF

these walls: St Antoninus, the first archbishop of Florence — a delicious bust of him in terracotta will be seen later — Savonarola and Fra Bartolomeo.

The protection of Eugenius IV and Cosimo il Vecchio enabled Dominicans from Fiesole to establish themselves in this monastery formerly occupied by followers of St Sylvester and reconstructed and enlarged by Michelozzo between 1437 and 1452. They began by restoring and decorating their church, which attracts little notice from tourists. Such neglect is rather unfair. Two tomb slabs record the names of Angelo Poliziano and Pico della Miràndola and a side-altar offers an eighth-century mosaic originating from the old basilica of St Peter in Rome. In it an unexpected glimpse of the Byzantine world is provided by the Virgin who is shown in imperial costume as she kneels in prayer.

But it is the cloister, cells and library of the convent itself, from which, alas, the monks departed in 1866, that absorb one's complete attention. The architectural style of the *quattrocento*, simple, graceful yet supremely professional, is seen here in its most monastic form, and the luminous art of Fra Angelico is encountered at every step. One of the first frescoes — a lunette — in the cloister of St Antoninus with its spreading cedar tree shows a monk who, finger to his lips, indicates the rule of silence. A rule which the visitor too should observe for Fra Angelico can best be understood and appreciated in a monachal silence. In any case all thought of speech evaporates before the huge *Crucifixion* in the chapter-house at the end of this cloister. You are precipitated into the tragic atmosphere of the Redemption by the variously meditating figures who

represent the founders of religious orders and other saintly personages. The contemplative St Dominic fixes his whole mind and heart upon the Cross; St Francis, his high-cheekboned face bronzed by sun and the open air, shares, in his own suffering, the Passion of Christ. This study of deep and universal sorrow beneath the ominous darkness of the sky has an unfailing beauty. 'He needs innocent faces and graceful forms,' wrote Suarès, 'and he finds them even in scenes of torture.' This impression is confirmed by the arresting *Deposition* in the Pilgrims' Hospice at the entrance to the cloister. What a contrast to the ravishing and much-loved *Madonna of the Star* seen in this same room where the monk's pictures are exhibited. In it the angel musicians form a joyous dancing aureole about the Mother of the Saviour.

The monks' cells are on the first floor, and one of the most moving experiences Florence can offer awaits you in the first of San Marco's two *Annunciations* which is seen on the landing. It is difficult to decide between Mary, in her utter humility, and the reverent though divine appearance of the heavenly messenger; between the new sense of space, the essential purity of the architecture, and the subtle variety of the colouring — a hymn to unity in itself. The *Annunciation* in the third cell is an even more perfect, more inward conception. For in each cell there is a fresco illustrating a scene from the New Testament, and in almost every case Fra Angelico put a monk at the base of the composition because these pictures were intended to aid the occupant in his daily meditation. How fortunate were those

SAN MARCO: ANGEL MUSICIANS,
BY FRA ANGELICO

who passed their monastic lives at San Marco; not many in this world enjoy such encouragement to prayer....

Concise yet filled with reverent majesty, these works do not follow a preconceived plan, being wholly personal in intention. The *Noli Me Tangere* preceded the *Annunciation*. In another chamber the *Purification* is depicted. Note the veneration expressed in the central figure, Simeon, holding the infant Jesus in his arms. The slim, nervous hands of the Madonna go out to her Child, and maternal anxiety is written in her face.

The *Descent into Limbo* in the cell of St Antoninus conveys the thrill of the Easter Eve liturgy. Christ strides along, 'his robes stirred by the wind: he is the figure of spring, of joy, of day itself, of divine ecstasy, passing through the gap that has opened up in the rocks!' (Boylesve). If only there were space to describe everything... the amazed adoration of the *Women at the Tomb*, the intoxicating *Transfiguration*, the *Coronation of the Virgin*. In these peaceful surroundings time stands still — eternity is before us.

A short distance from here is the Via Cavour, noisy and remarkable only for the Palazzo Riccardi, a building of massive strength surmounted by a sharply projecting cornice. In the days of the principality it was the residence of the Medici and should have continued to bear their name even though it changed hands in the seventeenth century. In this stately palace which witnessed many dramatic scenes Cosimo il Vecchio received the scholars who had been driven out of Byzantium by the Turks; Capponi, in the course of negotiations with Charles VIII, provoked him with the famous remark: 'Sound your trumpets and we will ring our bells!'; Alessandro de' Medici died here by the hand of his cousin.... It is also the official centre of the Tuscan

PALAZZO MEDICI-RICCARDI

language which, after prolonged and learned discussion, was recognized as the real language of the peninsula and not just a dialect: the Accademia della Crusca, founded in the sixteenth century, used to have its headquarters here. This organization was dedicated to the task of sifting the chaff from the wheat in the Italian language — its very name is a direct allusion to this — and spent many years working on the dictionary.

A collection of Medici portraits is housed on the ground floor. That of Lorenzo the Magnificent offers a striking contrast to his death mask which is also here; the anonymous artist made no concession to his noble subject who is shown in all his powerful ugliness. There is, too, a splendid portrait by Clouet of Catherine de' Medici wearing an indescribable farthingale studded with gems.

Apart from the inner courtyard which is also by Michelozzo, the chief interest of the palace lies in the frescoes of the tiny chapel: gorgeous and delightful scenes that were executed in 1463 by Benozzo Gozzoli in which, after the fashion of the time, he obligingly included a portrait of himself (the figure with *opus Benotii* on its hat). The subject, which is entirely conventional, is supposed to be the *Procession of the Magi to Bethlehem*, but this is no more than a pretext for a marvellous portrayal of his more illustrious contemporaries in Florence including, of course, the Medici. The figure of a bearded, fiercely handsome prince has been taken to represent the Emperor John VII Palaeologus, who appears on one of Pisanello's portrait-medals. He had attended the Oecumenical Council in Florence in 1439 and it seems likely that Gozzoli's symphonic composition was inspired by his memories of the solemn procession that ended this assembly and was a general source of wonder in his youth. His work shows more pomp and splendour than piety, with great psychological penetration and unrivalled craftsmanship.

The somewhat conventional orientalism which characterizes it recalls earlier works seen in the Uffizi. René Schneider has noted that 'tendency to cool gardens dotted with tiny flowers', that 'perspective rising so steeply that only a narrow strip of sky is left', and suggests that these traits may stem from the Persian miniatures of which there were known to be some specimens in the Medici collections. For all that, these angels and their Paradise seem a little insipid after Fra Angelico.

Between the Palazzo Riccardi and the little church of San Giovannino (which belongs to the *Scolopi*, a teaching order founded by St Joseph Calasanz) is the Via de' Gori which brings one in a few seconds to the Piazza San Lorenzo. This quarter is very busy indeed during the week with its popular and permanent market presided over by a statue of Giovanni delle Bande Nere that is far from bellicose: in fact, rather feeble.

The façade of San Lorenzo, like that of the Carmine, is of rough brick — *rozza*. Its bareness, although preferable to the ornate facing added to the Duomo and Santa Croce, must still give grounds for regret that Michelangelo never realized his project (an instructive model of this by Baccio d'Agnolo can be seen in the Casa Buonarroti). Michelangelo's sole achievement here is the decoration of the interior façade.

San Lorenzo is a particularly venerable church — *caput ecclesiarium florentinarum* — having been founded in the fourth century and consecrated by St Ambrose in person. Since then it has been destroyed, rebuilt and repaired several times. What has survived is a basilica by Brunelleschi with a coffered ceiling in the antique style but considerably altered after the architect's death. The luminous interior is of *pietra serena*. It is a memorable sight during the ceremonies of Good Friday evening when the only lighting is focused on the great crucifix by Baccio da Montelupo and a Madonna of the Sorrows — a figure of poignant simplicity with her downcast eyes — which stand on the starkly plain altar of sombre marble.

At the end of the right aisle is a *tabernacolo* by Desiderio da Settignano which was copied by numerous sculptors in the *quattrocento* and adds a graceful touch to this otherwise austere church. The principal and side aisles have works by Donatello here and there. The two pulpits standing near the crossing were executed at the very end of his life and are a little disappointing; the decorative bronze reliefs are confused and over-elaborate, characterized by a melodramatic excess of sorrow and 'an almost unbearable excitement' (A. Chastel).

The tomb of Cosimo il Vecchio under the entrance to the choir is often overlooked and, in fact, despite its fascination this church is of less interest to visitors than its annexes. The agreeably proportioned Old Sacristy has associations with Brunelleschi, who built it, Donatello, who decorated it, and Verrocchio who in 1472 designed the sarcophagus of two members of the Medici family which reveals an entirely new conception of funerary art. Before entering the more famous New Sacristy, take a look at the extraordinary Chapel of the Princes which was constructed on the axis of the choir of San Lorenzo, shortening it appreciably. This curious mausoleum, very high and surmounted by a cupola but no lantern, was begun by Fernando I who intended it for his own remains and those of his successors — a kind of Escorial or Saint-Denis for the grand dukes of Florence. From top to bottom the walls are faced with marble and alabaster, chalcedony, lapis lazuli, agate, and jasper, the main shades being green and dark red. Niches hold sarcophagi of porphyry. But only two of the gigantic statues of gilded bronze are actually in place, and the emptiness of the other recesses with their dead lying beneath in macabre solitude echoes the emptiness of the throne itself.

The other Medici chapel of San Lorenzo is, thanks to Michelangelo, completely different again in appearance though it too was left unfinished. By a paradox that was in keeping with the fate that dogged the master, the tomb of Lorenzo the Magnificent and his brother Giuliano was

CHAPEL IN THE PALAZZO MEDICI-RICCARDI: PARADISE, BY BENOZZO GOZZOLI (DETAIL)

not taken beyond the first draft, while that of Leo X was never even begun. The Lorenzo and Giuliano seen here, nephew and brother respectively of Leo X, were merely namesakes of their illustrious ancestors. They both died young, at twenty-seven and thirty-seven respectively, and but for Buonarroti most of us would have been ignorant of their unremarkable lives. As with so many others of his statues, Michelangelo made use of these figures to express general concepts: of these two dukes of Nemours and Urbino 'he made one into Action, the other into Thought' (R. Rolland). The antithesis is obvious. On one side the young warrior in his helmet, Lorenzo — *Il Pensieroso*, sits in sombre meditation. On the other Giuliano, holding his staff of command, muscles taut beneath his cuirass, is ready to move. And, of

156

CHAPEL IN THE PALAZZO MEDICI-RICCARDI : PROCESSION

THE MAGI TO BETHLEHEM, BY BENOZZO GOZZOLI

course, this contrast between the contemplative and active lives was a frequent theme of mediaeval art.

The four nude figures that flank the tombs are less straightforward to interpret. Action takes shape with the Day, at which Giuliano is gazing, and subsides at Night. Contemplation wavers more between the uncertain hours of Dawn and Twilight. The masculine figures, symbols of a tragic impotence, were left unfinished. Night and Dawn, which the sculptor did complete, are astounding fragments. The former can truly be said

AGI TO BETHLEHEM, BY BENOZZO GOZZOLI

to be 'not rare but unique'
(Vasari). The absurd
position, which wrinkles
and distorts the abdomen,
has caused a dispropor-
tionate development of
the thigh. The undeniable
vulgarity of the massive
body and the accom-
panying tragic mask and
owl have a nightmarish
effect; for in all this
Michelangelo was giving
expression to his own
despair when Florence
lost its liberty in 1532.
Dawn too conveys un-
bearable sadness. 'Her
indestructible beauty is
untouched,' said Taine,
'and yet her inner suffer-

THE THREE SISTERS OF
LORENZO THE MAGNIFICENT

ing is beginning to taint it. The superb
animal vigour, the tenacious power of muscle
and trunk are unimpaired, but the spirit is
failing…. How sad it is to waken again to
the knowledge that the burden of yet
another human day lies before one !'

It would be impossible to leave San
Lorenzo without visiting the cloister (1447),
which is reminiscent of Brunelleschi. At
night all that is visible of the town from
here is the top of the Campanile and the
cupolone in a glow of floodlight on the one
hand and, in half darkness, the noble façade
of the Laurentian Library on the other. In
the daytime this library is reached through
the cloister, from which a staircase built by
Vasari although designed by Michelangelo

SELF-PORTRAIT, BY GOZZOLI

leads up to the great chamber. Michelangelo undertook its construction in 1524 for Pope Clement VII who wanted a repository for the Medici collection of manuscripts; today these number about eight million including 180 of Dante's works and some wonderfully illuminated vellums. Certain of these volumes, like the Syriac gospel of the sixth century, are extremely archaic. This library has attracted scholars from all over the world since the sixteenth century. When Paul-Louis Courier spilt some ink on a manuscript of *Daphnis and Chloe* he had come to consult, he was in despair — and deep disgrace with the experts.

The Laurenziana is only one of the excellent libraries owned by this city that was indeed the Athens of the Renaissance. Another, the Marucelliana, which was founded at the end of the seventeenth century, is famous for its collection of engravings. The Riccardiana, too, with its 4,000 manuscripts, the medical library of Santa Maria Nuova and many more can be added to the list which is capped in this century by the ugly but large and well-planned building (between the Arno and Santa Croce) of the Biblioteca Nazionale, one of the most comprehensive and active libraries in all Italy.

It takes very little time to get from San Lorenzo to Santa Maria Novella. This vast church, the first sight to greet the visitor stepping on to the platform of the near-by railway station, cannot, with its annexes and

SAN LORENZO: MARBLE ESCUTCHEON
IN THE CHAPEL OF THE PRINCES

the treasures of its cloisters, be explored in a hurry. The tour that began at Santa Croce will find a satisfying conclusion here, for that great Franciscan sanctuary has its counterpart in this Dominican church which, like it, dates from the end of the thirteenth century.

For a first view of Santa Maria Novella, it is best to find a vantage-point — a porch, perhaps — on the other side of the square, now transformed into a public garden, where two small obelisks commemorate the

SAN LORENZO: TOMB OF GIULIANO DE' MEDICI, BY MICHELANGELO,
IN THE NEW SACRISTY

Roman-style chariot races which took place in the time of the grand dukes on the eve of the solemn feast of 24 June. Sad to say, one's enjoyment of this view is marred by the heavy flow of traffic in this area which is also the terminus of five bus services. A better position is the centre of the piazza itself, among the children and pigeons. Cypresses would have no place here and were done away with. The green-painted stall which is a permanent feature can be ignored.

There before you is the most beautiful church front in Florence. This composition seeming to partake of both architecture and music was the fantastic creation of Leon Battista Alberti in the mid fifteenth century. The work was commissioned by that great patron Giovanni Rucellai whose name is displayed in handsome Roman lettering below the fronton. The marble facing with its geometrical designs is obviously derived from the Romanesque and there are traces of Gothic in the lower part which, apart from the main doorway (by Alberti), was erected very early in the *trecento*. Visually, however, the effect is far from mediaeval. This recreation in the classical style by one of the most striking personalities of the fifteenth-century Renaissance provided an innovation in the two large scrolls connecting the two stages that was to be successfully adapted by baroque art.

Beyond the marble façade is hidden the neutral fabric of the church itself. All that can be seen from here is the graceful brick campanile of the fourteenth century which stands against the transept. The disparity is by no means offensive. When the sun is low the diffused golden light sheds a glory on brick and marble alike, while unending flocks of pigeons, hardly distinguishable against the similar colouring of the façade, whirl upwards to their nests : here is such vigour and plenitude, as well as grace, as is remarkable even in Florence.

The interior is majestic, with Gothic arches recalling the Duomo. The mere statement of its dimensions — 325 feet long and over 200 feet wide at the transept — shows that this space was designed to hold with ease the enormous congregations who came to hear the Dominicans preach. Under the high altar, which is modern though conforming to the traditional Florentine style (the tabernacle echoes Brunelleschi's dome), lies the body of the blessed John of Salerno who first brought the Dominican friars to this city.

The chief attraction of Santa Maria Novella for the art historian lies in the frescoes of the choir. The work of Domenico Ghirlandaio (1485-1490), these are yet another instance of the literally inexhaustible resources of the Florentine nobles at the climax of their ascendancy. The Medici were celebrated by Benozzo Gozzoli in the Palazzo Riccardi, the Bardi, Baroncelli, Peruzzi and Pazzi families were directly responsible for the art treasures of Santa Croce, the Pucci sponsored the porch of the Santissima Annunziata, the Rucellai provided the façade of this church; and the frescoes in its choir were an extravagant gesture on the part of the Tornabuoni, whose fortunes had reached their peak with the marriage of Lucrezia Tornabuoni to Piero il Gottoso, son of Cosimo il Vecchio.

The rare perfection of this pictorial group is spoiled by the sheer hypocrisy of its motive. The lives of St John the Baptist on one wall and of the Virgin on the other have been given an entirely conventional treatment: the artist's real intention was to do honour to the family which had bestowed this commission upon him, and their clients as well. The donors themselves, Giovanni Tornabuoni and his wife Francesca Pitti, are shown on the end wall, in the customary attitude of prayer. Several scenes, such as the *Visitation* to the right, and *Joachim Driven from the Temple* to the left, are cluttered with anachronistic figures whose presence destroys all religious feeling. How different from Giotto's treatment of the same subjects at Padua — bare, succinct, with a scrupulous consideration for unity of action. The Palazzo Riccardi demonstrated this tendency in the men of the high Renaissance to mingle their interpretation of sacred episodes with mundane chronicles of a rather shocking nature. In depicting on the walls of Santa Maria Novella the haughty figures of Ludovica Tornabuoni and Ginevra Benci, blonde and disdainful in their stiff, formal dresses, Ghirlandaio was obeying the frivolous dictates of the Florence of his time. Yet that must be a cause of satisfaction rather than reproach for, as a result, the portraits of some of the greatest humanists stand here today: Politian, unusually precocious poet and tutor of Leo X; Marsilio Ficino, the canon who endeavoured to reconcile the two philosophies of Plato and St Thomas Aquinas; Demetrios Chalcondylas, talking amicably to Politian who was in fact no friend of his....

This church enables one to grasp the peculiarities of the Christian outlook at the dawn of the sixteenth century. When, eighty years later, the unfortunate Veronese allowed himself still greater liberties — 'those taken by poets and madmen,' he said — he was summoned before the Holy Office and very sensibly given to understand by the judges that the first object of a religious picture was to aid the faithful in their devotions. Accordingly the artists of the Counter-Reformation made a much belated effort to correct the aberrations of which Ghirlandaio had already left a sensational example.

The huge church contains many other works which deserve to be considered at length. In a chapel adjacent to the choir is Filippino Lippi's *Raising of Drusiana* which invites comparison with Giotto's version in Santa Croce, while the same artist's *Miracle of St Philip* directly opposite calls for close study. The brilliance and dazzling technique of these two pictures are as astonishing as their flamboyant character. The confusion of archaeological details which cumber the theme resulted from the current infatuation with classical art, still a new revelation and imperfectly understood as yet. The gracefully charming tomb by Rossellino belongs to the same *genre*.

Much more serious in intent are Orcagna's very well-known retable, the *Pala Strozzi*, Vasari's reverent *Virgin of the Rosary* and the gigantic frescoes in the fourteenth-century Strozzi Chapel at the end of the left transept. Due to improvements in the lighting, these representations of *The Last Judgment*, *Hell* and *Paradise* by Nardo di Cione (about 1360) can now be seen much more clearly; perhaps similar innovations will enable the *Rucellai Madonna* to be brought back from its present home in the Uffizi and displayed in this church once more.

The Chiostro Verde is the most interesting of the cloisters round the former monastery. It takes its name from the prevailing tone of the mural decorations. Even in their damaged state, some of these frescoes offer a portrayal of Genesis that is both epic and realistic; *The Deluge* and *The*

'IL PENSIEROSO'

DAWN

Sacrifice of Noah are by Paolo Uccello, the former containing more than a suggestion of Signorelli in its heroism and dramatic power.

From here one reaches the old chapter-house where divine service used to be held for the Castilian attendants of Eleanor of Toledo and which consequently became known as the Spanish Chapel. The great Gothic vaults and the walls are entirely covered with frescoes by Andrea da Firenze (1355) which were restored in 1750. The theme is thought to have been suggested to the painter by the prior of the monastery, Iacopo Passavanti, author of a book entitled *Speculum Verae Poenitentiae*, and is in fact the glorification of the Dominican Order, showing on one side its activities in the Church Militant. White dogs with black spots — *domini canes*, a terrible pun! — tear the heretics to pieces and frisk about the flock of faithful Christians they are guarding. By means of the confessional, the preaching friars snatch mankind away from terrestrial pleasures and guide them towards the glory and eternal joys of heaven. Some art critics have taken candour so far as to identify one of the young women symbolizing earthly temptations (on the right) as Petrarch's Laura — although nobody knows what she really looked like.

Opposite is the portrayal of the Church Triumphant, unappealing in its conscious and inflexible authority. St Thomas Aquinas is enthroned above Arius and two other arch-heretics, all three abashed by the *Summa contra Gentiles*. The three theological and the four cardinal virtues hover, wings spread, in the atmosphere. On either side of the great teacher are shown ten patriarchs, prophets and apostles. At his feet fourteen female figures on heavy Gothic thrones personify the liberal arts and sciences on which mediaeval knowledge was based.

166

COURTYARD OF THE CHIOSTRO VERDE

Beneath each of these is seen the outstanding practitioner or representative. Euclid for geometry, Clement V for canon law, Justinian for civil law and so on. The composition of these four stages around St Thomas (three, four, ten, fourteen) corresponds with the gradual enlargement of the surface contained by one of the four Gothic arches supporting the vault. St Thomas himself would surely have approved of this disposition for it matches his own system of thought. The other two walls are devoted to the *Crucifixion* and the *Life of St Peter Martyr*.

It is not far from Santa Maria Novella to Santa Trinità, to which connoisseurs of Ghirlandaio will inevitably be drawn. But instead of going straight there, it is worth making a detour. If possibly temporary solutions to the traffic problem in Florence are of interest to you, go and see what is being done in the Via de' Cerretani, with its ingenious system of paths for pedestrians. The construction of subways has been suggested but, judging by those in Rome, might prove an expensive project.

The narrow side streets are cool and relatively quiet, and one of them, the Via della Vigna Nuova, contains another example of Leon Battista Alberti's work, the Palazzo Rucellai. The inventive powers

SANTA MARIA NOVELLA: THE SACRIFICE OF ZACHARIAS, BY GHIRLANDAIO.
DETAIL: SOME MEMBERS OF THE TORNABUONI FAMILY

demonstrated in his façade for Santa Maria Novella were given full play in this secular building too, with its walls relieved by the numerous windows and inset pilasters.

Another handsome residence, earlier in date, is the Palazzo Antinori, recalling similar patrician houses in Siena and now occupied by the British Institute. It stands opposite the baroque church of San Gaetano at the beginning of the Via Tornabuoni and a few yards from the Via de' Cerretani.

SANTA MARIA NOVELLA: THE BIRTH OF ST JOHN, BY GHIRLANDAIO (DETAIL)

The Via Tornabuoni is the most fashionable street in Florence, and in it can be found the principal foreign consulates, leading jewellers and florists, and the chief bookshops.

This street is dominated by the formidable presence of the Palazzo Strozzi which, with the Riccardi, is one of the largest *palazzi* — the Pitti apart — in Florence and probably the most astonishing of them all. Many famous names are associated with it, for several members of this great family gave invaluable service to France and the founder of it received such men as Rabelais and the Cardinal du Bellay. Equally well known were its architects : Benedetto da Maiano who began work on it in 1489;

THE CHURCH MILITANT (DETAIL)   SANTA MARIA NOVELLA: CAPPELLONE DEGLI

Cronaca, the designer (before 1507) of the splendid cornice, annoyingly left unfinished and rivalling that of the Palazzo Farnese in Rome; and

SPAGNUOLI (ANDREA DA FIRENZE)   TRIUMPH OF ST THOMAS AQUINAS

PALAZZO STROZZI

finally Caparra, so called in Italian because before executing any commission he always demanded a substantial advance, who created the wrought-iron lanterns at the corners and the torch-holders. From the little Piazza Strozzi behind the palace can be seen the finest of its three façades. The skill of the builder is apparent in the way that the embossment, which is very prominent at ground level, is gradually reduced in the upper storeys, a device which lessens the oppressive effect of the building. The austere inner courtyard by Cronaca is much renowned.

The end of the Via Tornabuoni widens into the triangle marked by the Column of Justice brought from the Baths of Caracalla in Rome and presented to Cosimo I by Pope Pius IV. This piazza is named after the church of Santa Trinità which stands here. Yet another contrast between a seventeenth-century façade and a Gothic interior of remarkable purity, undoubtedly the oldest example of this style in Florence. Innumerable frescoes adorned the walls of this beautiful building but only traces of them remain today; such as the tenderly depicted scenes from the life of the Magdalene, attributed to Puccio Capanna, Giotto's disciple and collaborator in the upper church at Assisi. Lorenzo Monaco is also represented here. But it is again Ghirlandaio who carries the day with his work in the funeral Sassetti chapel containing a wonderfully designed tomb. The painter's choice of theme is in itself of little importance. In *The Approval of the Franciscan Rule by Honorius III* various witnesses are posed well to each side of the composition or are shown making a theatrical entrance from a staircase. Some of the figures can be identified as Lorenzo the Magnificent with his young sons, including the future Pope Leo X, and their tutor, already encountered in Santa Maria Novella. There is no apparent reason for their presence here; but no doubt the painter was obliged to follow the caprices of his times or to further Lorenzo's ambitious designs.

The relics of St John Gualberto are preserved in this church, as well as the crucifix which according to tradition leaned towards him one Good Friday at San Miniato. A few minutes beforehand the young noble had come face to face with the murderer of his brother and was just about to run him through; then abruptly forgave him for the love of Christ on the Cross. Later he campaigned against the simony which raged throughout Tuscany in the untamed eleventh century, earning in his own lifetime the glorious title of 'liberator of Italy'.

The Piazza Santa Trinità is also associated with the terrible clashes of 1302 which brought victory to the Blacks and misery to Dante Alighieri. At this point a choice of two completely different routes presents itself. You can make for the Via Por Santa Maria and the Ponte Vecchio, passing through the Borgo Santi Apostoli with its sombre, towering *palazzi* of which a large number date from the thirteenth century or even earlier. Standing on a quiet and very ancient little piazza is the small and irresistible

Romanesque church of the Santi Apostoli. However, the traditional belief (perpetuated by the plaque on the façade) that Charlemagne himself saw it being built is quite unfounded and should be ignored.

As to the Via Por Santa Maria, the least said the better, so dismal is the effect of the recent reconstruction. The sole survivors are the mediaeval towers, freed from the screen of *palazzi* which had grown up round them only to fall victim to worse; they must feel as out of place in this new setting as a Cimabue in a Cubist exhibition.

If you decided to follow the Lungarno Corsini in the direction of the Cascine on the west side of the town, you will have noticed the palace built in the seventeenth century for the wealthy Corsini family which, through its later close connection with the papacy, became one of the most powerful in Italy. In the state apartments of this magnificent residence hundreds of paintings by the most diverse artists from Memling to Guido Reni and Guercino provide a supplement to the Pitti collections. The way then lies along the fashionable Borgo Ognissanti into the piazza of the same name. Originally this was called after Daniele Manin, but when the Fascist regime discovered the Semitic origins of that Venetian patriot it restored the piazza to All Saints and a group by Romano Romanelli was substituted for Manin's statue which was banished to the Viale de' Colli.

The church of Ognissanti, with its slender campanile, looks on to the Arno; the *Coronation of the Virgin* seen on the tympanum of its door is by a pupil of the Della Robbia. If you have already seen the *cenacolo* here, go straight into the Franciscan church; among its frescoed Doctors of the Church, Botticelli's *St Augustine* can be identified beyond doubt and also Domenico Ghirlandaio's *St Jerome*, in which the books are painted with a precision and care for detail more characteristic of the Flemish school.

Before leaving the church and piazza, spare a glance for the Palazzo Pisani, a very typical early fifteenth-century edifice with its huge cornice and picturesque corbels. This palace belongs to France and is occupied by the French Institute in Florence, which was founded by the University of Grenoble.

The time has come to close the guide-book for today and find somewhere to relax. The Orto Botanico, for instance, close by San Marco and the University? Or the cypress-grown English Cemetery in the Piazzale Donatello, where the charming Elizabeth Barrett Browning lies? Beyond the pleasantly shaded *viali* which encircle Florence in their progress from one to another of the old gates, all that remains of the city wall of 1284, roads disappear into the outskirts. 'At the end of a street lying in warm shadow one's eyes rest on a round-backed mountain' (Taine).

As the day draws to a close it is amusing to watch the younger Florentines enjoying themselves. This is the hour when all along the Corso, from the Via del Proconsolo to the Piazza della Repubblica, they parade incessantly up and down and back again, in much the same way as in so many other Mediterranean towns — Palermo, Barcelona, Oran, Palma, Ajaccio, or Aix-en-Provence. In the passage connecting the Via dell' Oriuolo with the Borgo degli Albizzi the air is fragrant with the olive oil that the sellers of *bomboloni* use for frying these jam fritters. Whichever street you are in you find the same throngs of passers-by, the same urchins chasing across from one pavement to the other, and hundreds of bicycles, Lambrettas and Vespas as they dive into the strolling crowds — already

SANTA TRINITÀ: THE DEATH OF
ST FRANCIS OF ASSISI, BY GHIRLANDAIO (DETAIL)

in danger from the stream of vehicles — dextrously winding in and out at top speed. How full of life and bustle these streets are. Less crude than the old quarter of Marseilles, less exotic than an Eastern bazaar, but varying with the seasons and the time of day. Do you recall the bewilderment of the ineffable Sylvestre Bonnard as he disembarked at a Sicilian port? 'I am listening, my friend,' he said to the seller of water-

SANTA TRINITÀ: THE APPROVAL OF THE FRANCISCAN

OPE HONORIUS III, BY GHIRLANDAIO

FLORENCE AT NIGHT

melons. He would find his brother here, behind one of the numerous *carretini* loaded with fruit.

The shop fronts as night falls become a dazzle of glaring lights. At eight or half past the citizens of Florence decide, with some indifference, to go out to dinner. The time has come to choose a scene of gastronomic activity. The *ristoranti* which make a display of gleaming silver-plate for the tourists with well-lined pockets are to be avoided. Try a *trattoria* instead, or better still a *mescita di vini* or wine shop with a few tables in the corner where meals are served. The satisfying skill shown in the arrangement of the bottles and the politeness of the attendant who has, however, too much natural dignity to be obsequious are pleasurable features here.

Before a mound of common spaghetti or *lasagne alla bolognese*, with some Chianti as dark as ink beside him, the tourist ceases to be conscious of the activity of the street which is in any case subsiding. His steak is sizzling on the grill, cooked to perfection as only Florentine restaurateurs know how to do it in all Italy. '*Al sangue?*' asks the waiter, while the puzzled customer is absorbed in reading an incredibly long list, trying to find out what dishes he can have.

Even in such circumstances it is rewarding to watch the Tuscan faces which may be seen at a near-by table, faces animated by conversation. If your Italian is good enough, ask for some information about life in the city, the approaching festival. You may get an uncertain or inaccurate answer, but it will have a racy tang and be delivered with agreeable charm. From such slight acquaintances lifelong friendships can grow.

A TRATTORIA

SAN MINIATO AL MONTE

PORTA SAN GIORGIO

OLTR'ARNO

I N a town as compact as Florence the Arno valley provides welcome air
and space. A group of corbelled houses which date from the middle
ages are still standing, having escaped the destruction of 1944, with their
foundations deep in the often muddy waters. The *lungarni* (quays) enable
those living in the city to enjoy a breath of air on summer nights or the
benevolent warmth of the sun — the *termosifone del povero* or the poor
man's stove — in winter. The foreign visitor returning here after some

years will be struck by the incredible narrowness of the *lungarno* between the Uffizi and the Ognissanti; both pavement and roadway seem woefully inadequate for the flow of traffic today. And there is no remedy for this

SHOPS ON THE PONTE VECCHIO

state of affairs. It would be impossible to displace the *palazzi* bordering it on the landward side.

Yet in out-of-season periods it can still be pleasant to walk along here in the early morning when peace reigns once more, with the spectacle of this Tuscan river before one and beyond it the fine view of the campaniles, gardens and hills on the left bank.

It is hard to choose visually between the two famous bridges that invite the tourist to cross the Arno; both are attractive though utterly dissimilar. The Ponte Vecchio, which was constructed at the narrowest point of the river, fully deserves this name — 'the old bridge'; mention of it is found in records from the year 996 onwards. It was rebuilt in the middle of the fourteenth century, following a serious flood, probably under the supervision of the architect who designed the staircase in the Bargello. The jewellers' and goldsmiths' shops which are crowded on to it practically from one end to the other had already been established there by the late middle ages. Of all Florence this spot is perhaps better known than any other to foreigners, if only by repute, and it figures in the plans and dreams of honeymoon couples. Literature, too, is full of allusions to the Ponte Vecchio.

Small squares of mosaic, where fiery-tinted birds of marble fly out from a dark background, silver filigree necklaces and other articles, whimsically designed rings and tiny, fanciful boats, coral in every shape and form; little spoons in silver gilt tipped with the figure of Verrocchio's boy with a dolphin; bracelets, brooches and pins of the most imaginative, even fantastic, design. Alongside charming trinkets like these, other jewellery of a much inferior type is on sale to less discerning customers. The Ponte Vecchio, however, is not the only place where these marvellous creations by the goldsmiths of Florence can be bought, for similar shops are to be found along the *lungarni*, in the centre of the city itself, and from the Via de' Guicciardini to the Palazzo Pitti on the left bank.

The actual structure of the bridge was dangerously affected by the blowing up of its supporting points in 1944, particularly those on the Via de' Guicciardini side, for the problems of reconstruction here could not easily be resolved. In recent years the piers had to be entirely reinforced, even to their foundations in the river bed. The loveliest of all the bridges on the Arno, the Ponte Santa Trinità, was also a victim of those war-time ravages. Once more it can be seen in the form that Bartolomeo Ammannati planned for it in 1566. The reconstruction, only just completed, was made possible by a public appeal for funds among whose distinguished supporters were men and women whose names already belong to the history of civilization. This *cinquecento* masterpiece is an everlasting joy to see; the elongated arches of grey-brown stone are each finished with a keystone of white marble, and these too are reflected in the glistening waters. The centre curve, 'supple as the bow of a god' (Vaudoyer), is imperceptibly higher than the rest.

A single detail is missing from the decoration of this bridge and will remain so for an indefinite period. It is impossible not to notice that the most celebrated of the four statues of the *Seasons* which stand guard, one on either side, at each end is without its head. The figure of *Flora* (Spring) was damaged in the war, and though it was repaired and replaced with the utmost care the head could not be found, having been presumably carried off by persons unknown. Unless the original is recovered the statue will remain in its mutilated state, despite popular feeling instanced by graffiti on the pedestal which read : '*Cercasi testa anche usata*' — 'Wanted : a head, even if well worn'.

Whichever bridge you choose to take you to the other side, the important thing is to get there, for the churches to be found on the left bank do not deserve to be neglected.

There is no possible comparison between Santa Felicità, the little parish church of the grand dukes situated on the road to the Pitti and containing an unusual *Entombment* by Pontormo, and the immense church of Santo Spirito which was completed in the second half of the fifteenth century to the design of Brunelleschi. The sober, bare façade gives no hint of the excellence of its interior, built in *pietra serena*. The aisles, separated from the body of the nave by magnificent columns with Corinthian capitals, are prolonged to run right round the two arms of the transept and the choir itself. Works of art of great beauty adorn the thirty-eight chapels. The sacristy, which is surmounted by a cupola, was designed by Giuliano da San Gallo and Cronaca; the entrance vestibule, with its coffered vault and columns, is a convincing imitation of Roman architecture.

The situation of the church of the Carmine (Carmelites) on the other side of the Via de' Serragli is rather out of the way. But it would be unpardonable to overlook the frescoes in one of its chapels for they have a unique interest for any student of Tuscan painting. Due to the carelessness of workmen engaged to repair the roof, the thirteenth-century structure was unfortunately burned down in January 1771, the transept chapels and the sacristy being all that escaped. Ten years later the Carmine had been rebuilt in the rococo style with white stucco walls; the vault of the nave was decorated with one of those elaborate compositions where crowds of cherubs hover against swelling clouds, the whole thing skilfully presented in a *trompe-l'œil* architectural framework to increase the depth of the perspective. Such a theatrical setting is rarely encountered in Florence and is in violent contrast here to the Brancacci chapel at the end of the south transept. The walls of this are covered with fifteen frescoes of the *quattrocento*, disposed in two stages. Taken in chronological order, the three earliest were executed in 1424 by Masolino da Panicale, seven others were done immediately afterwards by Masaccio, and the remainder by Filippino Lippi sixty years later. Masaccio, who died at the age of twenty-six, left little else than his frescoes here.

He was an amazingly precocious genius and innovator — one of those that leave posterity with the enigmatic question : what would they

PONTE SANTA TRINITÀ

have done if they had lived longer? This young artist is regarded as second only to Giotto in initiating the renascence of art in Italy, and like the latter he overthrew all the principles which had been accepted up to that time. Time and time again critics have insisted that the work of Signorelli, for example, or even Michelangelo cannot be explained without close study of Masaccio's frescoes in the Carmine and understanding of their implications.

His master was Masolino, a native of the Val d'Elsa, who appears to have been an extremely fashionable painter, for he was invited to do work as far afield as Hungary shortly after painting the *Temptation* in the Brancacci chapel : two nudes of such beauty — especially Eve — that

they really do conjure up a new world of which the artists of the *trecento* had no conception.

But Masaccio demonstrates a much greater mastery in his *Expulsion from Paradise* which is directly opposite: a mastery compounded of his expression of feeling — Adam's shame, Eve's wailing despair; his expert construction; his modelling of forms — even to the suggestion of volume; his use of shadow; and the technical audacity of his foreshortened presentation of the Angel who points out the way to exile. The same qualities are noticeable in his scenes from the life of St Peter, particularly in *St Peter Healing the Sick with His Shadow* and, above all, in *The Tribute Money:* note the divine power, faith and hope expressed in the face of Christ and the

attitude of Peter. Space seems to have become tangible.

On emerging from the Carmine you may feel like a rest. The Villa Franchetti up at Bellosguardo offers an agreeable view over the town from its flower-grown terrace. Your way down again takes you past the Giardino di Boboli and shortly afterwards to the Palazzo Pitti. The architecture of this huge building should not be judged too hastily. The side facing the city is not attractive. It has strength and a certain austere majesty but it fails to charm, suggesting rather some gigantic prison. The stylistic balance of the original palace was destroyed by the addition of two enormous wings in the seventeenth and eighteenth centuries.

Begun in the fifteenth century for Luca Pitti who belonged to a very wealthy family antagonistic to Lorenzo de' Medici, this residence was eventually completed by Ammannati at the behest of the celebrated Eleanor of Toledo. This architect from Settignano was responsible for the inner courtyard with its two wings overlooking the Giardino di Boboli. Its harmonious construction shows the application in a more developed form of Brunelleschi's principles. Maria de' Medici was born and brought up in the central part of the palace which later inspired the

THE TEMPTATION OF ADAM AND EVE
BY MASOLINO DA PANICALE

design of the Luxembourg Palace in Paris. This task was given by Maria de' Medici to a famous French architect, Salomon de Brosse, and to please her he adopted the Tuscan style as it was represented by the Palazzo Pitti, where it is particularly noticeable in the façade looking on to the gardens. A characteristic feature of this style is the rusticated embossment already seen at the Palazzi Strozzi and Riccardi.

Victor Emmanuel II lived for a time in this former home of the grand dukes. Later, in 1919, it was surrendered by the Crown to the Ministry of Education which facilitated its establishment as a museum and centre of fine arts.

It may be that visitors exhausted by so many treasures will yearn for a quiet stroll on cool pleasant lawns : let them wander at will in the garden of the Medici. By its nature it belongs with the most famous and traditional gardens of Europe even though it lacks both the indescribable and monumental majesty of the Villa d'Este (slightly earlier in date) and the royal vastness of Versailles. In rather the same way as the park at Saint-Cloud, its layout embraces and exploits the hilly terrain : hence the variety of its aspects for the stroller and the unexpected glimpses of

ADAM AND EVE EXPELLED
FROM PARADISE, BY MASACCIO

the town through gaps in the screens of leaves. At the top of Boboli there is a small terrace off the beaten track of the more formal paths which provides a view of the Palazzo della Signoria in an unexpected setting.

Most impressive of all at Boboli, though, is the classical garden which recalls those of the villas at Frascati. The grassy amphitheatre — not too large — is crowned with a semicircular balustrade, and there are terracotta vases and copies of antique marbles, fountains and groves, against a background of evergreen oaks, cypresses, laurels and cedar trees. The Viottolone descends majestically and unwaveringly between dark walls of evergreen to the ornamental pool with its fountain by Giambologna. The Florentine character of this garden can be detected in certain of its aspects: its distinction and elegance; its dignity touched sometimes with disdain, sometimes with melancholy; its mystery, in short.

On the hillside above Boboli the magnificently laid-out Viale de' Colli follows its undulating course from east to west. The best way to see it is undoubtedly from a car, starting from the Porta Romana above the Royal Stables. The view over the city and over Fiesole changes from moment to moment, and the experience of seeing the now familiar shapes of churches and palaces in unfamiliar contexts is wholly fascinating.

For the pedestrian other routes suggest themselves, quieter and less troubled by motor traffic — which includes heavy lorries and scooters. Near Santa Felicità begins the rough and steep ascent of the Costa San Giorgio, with its rather gloomy working-class houses and broad-flagged

CARMINE: THE TRIBUTE MONEY, BY MASACCIO (DETAIL)

THE CHURCH OF SANTO SPIRITO

roadway, the loud voices of women and the laughter of children, and higher up sunny gardens and little baroque oratories. And suddenly, there is the ancient citadel of the Belvedere, where arms have given place to art; from the grassy terraces which were once its glacis, part of the town and the river can be seen with complete and uncompromising clarity. So it is agreeable to stop for a while under the Porta San Giorgio which has a fourteenth-century bas-relief of *St George and the Dragon* that contrives to be reverent and gay at the same time. The Via San Leonardo, meandering between the high walls of villas and offering occasional glimpses of their flower-filled gardens, passes the charming church whose name it bears; in this is found a wonderful thirteenth-century pulpit, a richly Romanesque work. The next halt can be either the Poggio Imperiale, the former residence of the grand duchesses and now a boarding school for the daughters of the aristocracy; or the Torre del Gallo, a small Ghibelline castle suffering from too much restoration but splendidly situated at a height of over 600 feet so that its tower is visible from everywhere roundabout — and was probably used by Galileo in the course of his experiments. The way now lies along the Via Giramonte in the direction of San Miniato and takes you among olive trees cascading down on every side. A magnificent grove of cypresses stands near the church itself; following the pious custom of the country, many of these trees were planted in memory of those who died in the 1914-18 war.

The basilica of San Miniato is, in my opinion, the finest example of Romanesque art in this region. Very ancient in its origins and containing the relics of the first Tuscan martyrs, the church dates, in its greater part, from the eleventh and twelfth centuries. After its completion at the beginning of the thirteenth, it remained more or less as it was during the following centuries. The marble-faced façade, with its geometrical designs and inset mosaic in the Byzantine style, forms part of an architectural group comprising the crenellated palace of the former bishops, the fortress based on Michelangelo's designs, and the thickset, massive campanile of the sixteenth century which stood up to the furious pounding of Charles V's cannon. This complex of buildings now serves as a monastery. The old cemetery, which still exists, in front of the church and to one side, is admirably situated. From it the eagle which surmounts the façade and betokens the art of Calimala stands out clearly.

No one coming to Florence should miss the opportunity of seeing the profoundly religious interior of this basilica. The double row of columns is interspersed with compound pillars, for a few diaphragm arches support the visible timber-work — repainted disastrously in the nineteenth century — of the central nave. One is struck by the subtlety of the light which seems to come less from the windows, small in themselves, than from the bright marble facing of the walls with their geometrical decorations; by the colour (the dark green marble of Prato) of the archstones; and by the monks' choir, raised well above the eleventh-century crypt. The marble furnishings (1207) are worthy of note, and the apse curving around the simple twelfth-century altar expresses a unity and purity that accord perfectly with the holy mysteries; the window openings are filled with translucent slabs. The mosaic (1291) in the apse is still completely Romanesque in spirit: Christ enthroned, surrounded by the four symbols of the Evangelists, between the Virgin and St Minias — portrayed as an Armenian prince. There is an obvious analogy with the Pantocrator in the Norman churches of Sicily.

It is tempting to linger over the mediaeval frescoes still to be seen in the aisles and, too, the marble pavement of the nave. At this point mention must be made of the importance and beauty of two fifteenth-century monuments : the altar in the nave, which became the chapel of the Crucifix because it was rebuilt by Michelozzo on the instructions of Piero il Gottoso to accommodate the famous crucifix of St John Gualberto, now at Santa Trinità, and the chapel of the Cardinal of Portugal in the left aisle. A pupil of Brunelleschi was responsible for the architectural style here, and Rossellino designed the tomb of James, grandson of John I of Portugal and Archbishop of Lisbon, who died suddenly in Florence around 1460 while in the prime of life. A smiling Madonna in a tondo and the figures adorning the funeral monument enhance by their sorrowful charm the youth and also the purity of the prelate.

Stop for a moment on the threshold of the basilica. Through the wide open door — where during Holy Week a young monk stands quietly awaiting your offering — there, like a picture in its frame, are the most celebrated sights of the old city : towers, campaniles, cupolas....

Hidden among the trees is the neighbouring church of San Salvatore al Monte, which Michelangelo liked to call his 'pretty country maid'. Gradually and irrevocably it is slipping down towards the town each year, this circumspect Franciscan church. The late fifteenth-century façade by Cronaca is extremely restrained as to ornament : the alternation of triangular and curved frontons for the windows was still, at that time, a novelty in architectural decoration. The double row of ancient cypresses lining the flight of steps that leads to the church increases the gravity of the setting. Something of the peaceful atmosphere of Assisi reigns here. After passing San Miniato and San Salvatore one after the other, the Viale de' Colli comes out into the Piazzale Michelangiolo which was laid out by the architect Giuseppe Poggi in 1874. The next year, to mark the fourth centenary of the birth of Michelangelo, the esplanade was adorned with a bronze reproduction of the *David* flanked by copies of the four nudes in the New Sacristy of San Lorenzo. The general effect is not successful; facility is verging on vulgarity. And why was this square made so vast and bare ? Was this really the best way to show off the boy athlete ? It seems rather to put him at a disadvantage.

Go down again from San Salvatore by the staircase called the Monte

GIARDINO DI BOBOLI

SAN SALVATORE AL MONTE

alle Croci (because of the Stations of the Cross which border it, leading finally to this church) and you will find yourself at the Porta San Miniato. To the left of this a comparatively well-preserved portion of the old city wall is still standing. It is a spot which somehow retains a strongly mediaeval atmosphere. But soon a turn in the street brings into view the opaque waters of the Arno turned to copper by the setting sun.

From the *lungarno* on the right bank, one's glance is drawn towards the hill. The mosaic of San Miniato glitters among the darkening cypresses in the old cemetery. Night has already come to the town below; but for a long time yet that façade will be lit by the last fiery rays of the sun.

SAN MINIATO AL MONTE: PULPIT

SANTA MARIA IMPRUNETA: THE TOWER

CASTELLO: THE VILLA DELLA PETRAIA

OUTSIDE FLORENCE

THERE is a choice of brief excursions outside the city limits, none of them taking more than half a day, that combine the pleasures of art with those of natural scenery, which is gentle and delicate here.

Beyond the Lungarno Amerigo Vespucci on the right bank of the Arno, going downstream, is a *piazzale* with a colossal equestrian statue of the founder of Italian unity, Victor Emmanuel II — an imperious figure against a curtain of green.

The trees in the background belong to the Cascine. This park, which skirts the river for well over two miles, has something of the character of the Bois de Boulogne in Paris and, like the latter, it contains an enormous race-course. The whole thing is fairly recent in date. Originally this site was occupied by farms and estates owned by the grand dukes and it was they who laid out the Cascine towards the end of the eighteenth century when 'English' gardens were becoming very popular. Nothing elaborate : just high thick copses and some stretches of grass. This is where worthy citizens spend Sunday afternoons in the bosom of their families. Around noon on a sunny winter's day the clatter of hooves can sometimes be heard. A group of young people, without their cars for once, lean their elbows on the parapet and argue about some weighty matter, while smart horsemen ride slowly past.

But these gardens are ordinary enough and it would be a waste of time to devote too much attention to them. After a cursory look at the

VILLA DI CASTELLO

bust of the Maharajah of Kolhapur whose death in Florence at the age of twenty oddly echoes that of the Cardinal of Portugal, make your way to the Porta al Prato and the road to Sesto Fiorentino. Since it is of course impossible to inspect all the handsome villas in the suburbs — many of them, in any case, are private property and not likely to be on view — you might pick two of the most notable which are fairly close to each other; both of them belonged at one time to the house of Savoy and, in the generous tradition of the Palazzo Pitti, their grounds are thrown open to the public. The atmosphere of Tuscany in the sixteenth and seventeenth centuries is vividly present in the Villa di Castello and the Villa della Petraia, and that sophisticated civilization which around the year 1600 influenced all Europe to a greater or lesser degree can be appreciated here in a more tangible form.

There is nothing beautiful about the approach to Castello. Since the restoration carried out in the eighteenth century the main building has lost the distinguished appearance it had in the time of the Medici. So the attraction here lies not in the villa but the garden, which is small enough to be taken in at one glance. But what skill and perfect judgment are shown in its proportions and layout. One might think everything was planned so as to set off Tribolo's fountain in the middle, which is surmounted by Ammannati's group of *Hercules and Cacus*. Everywhere classical sculptures mingle with neatly clipped trees and hedges of box. Castello was the prototype of Boboli, preceding it by twenty years, and may be regarded as one of the most delightful of the Italian gardens, in the horticultural sense, which were ultimately to inspire Le Nôtre.

Grottoes were much in vogue at the time of Cosimo I; Boboli has its share of them too. The one in the park here at Castello is huge and high; inside it bristles with stone stalactites, and gigantic figures of animals — including an elephant and a rhinoceros — make it a real zoo for small children. There is also a mischievous contraption that deluges visitors with water from jets which are turned on by their own footsteps (a joke dating from the middle ages and found in many other places than Florence). All of which makes it obvious that Castello is an extraordinary manifestation of a period that could be at the same time dramatic and puerile, uncouth and majestic.

Five minutes' walk along a hillside road separates the Villa di Castello from the one-time royal Villa della Petraia. The little palace, the garden in front of it and the park behind are, separately and together, all admirable. The Brunelleschi family once owned a castle on this site and put up a heroic resistance when besieged here by Sir John Hawkwood in 1364. The property, which occupies a magnificent strategic position commanding the valley, subsequently passed into the hands of various other families before it became a Medici possession. Cardinal Fernando de' Medici, who renounced the purple in order to succeed his brother as grand duke in 1587, had the villa completely altered, leaving only the tower as a reminder of the former building; he transformed the gardens too, wanting no doubt to equal the achievements at Tivoli of Cardinal Ippolito d'Este in the previous generation.

Inside, the villa presents some rather diverting contrasts. The great courtyard on the ground floor, for instance, with its richly colourful decoration of sumptuous frescoes by Volterrano (relatively unknown, these), was converted into a ballroom by Victor Emmanuel II by means of a glass roof supported by hideous iron stays.

Between the sloping garden and the mysterious park with its age-old trees the villa lies graciously at peace. On the topmost terrace is a fountain by Tribolo with a statue of *Venus* by Giambologna. The goddess is shown wringing the water from her hair, after her bath. Before her and below the basins with their murmuring, trickling waters, all Florence lies golden in the sun.

On the way back to the city the gardens surrounding the little Villa Stibbert should mark a halt. Frederick Stibbert, the son of an English father and Italian mother, was a collector and bequeathed to the city some of the rarest armour to be seen in Italy. Furniture, ceramics and various *objets d'art* complete this museum.

The villas that belonged originally to Lorenzo de' Medici may not be considered worth a visit. The Villa Medicea di Careggi, where he lived for most of the time and where he died, is jealously guarded. It is reserved for the use of nurses from Santa Maria Nuova, the hospital of Florence, but if and when this rest-home is transferred elsewhere the villa could be restored in a quite sensational way. At present the terraced gardens, once the site of Lorenzo's famous botanical park, are a sad sight. Unless something is done about them, the red lilies in pebble-work set into the paths will be entirely obliterated. The other villa, at Poggio a Caiano, stands on a slight eminence above the Ombrone, that miserable stream idealized by Lorenzo and his poet friends. The unpretentious park has been left to run wild. But even though the villa has been disfigured by the radical alterations to its staircase, it has an interesting peristyle that should not be overlooked. It is a perfect illustration of the Renaissance in Lorenzo's period with its coffered roof, unfinished fresco by Filippino Lippi and, below the pediment, the puzzling mythological frieze in majolica which has been variously interpreted of late by André Chastel and Warman Welliver and is open to explanation by everyone in their own way.

The trip to Settignano, on the other hand (by trolley-bus from the Piazza San Marco), can be recommended without reservation. There are few works of art here and no museums or libraries, with the exception of the villa owned by Bernard Berenson, the celebrated art critic, which he left to Harvard University. Sightseeing is confined to the beauties of nature, and so your mind can relax. Not as high up as Fiesole, this village from which sprang so many great sculptors of the Renaissance is gently moulded to its hill, lying on a slope that catches the abundant sunshine. It can be reached by the main road from Florence, lazily winding its way through the olive trees, or by the somewhat steep lanes from the direction of Rovezzano.

The village was badly damaged in the summer of 1944. Since that time the building and gardens of the Villa Gamberaia, nearly a mile beyond Settignano, have been completely and most successfully restored. This unassuming villa makes its first appearance as a flash of white through the silvery foliage of the olive trees which clothe the valley sides. Situated on a little promontory, it commands a superb panorama. The evergreen oaks, the rock garden and the terrace with its shining pools, the delicate colouring

CASTELLO: THE VILLA DELLA PETRAIA

of its flowers and the playing fountains are enchanting within their modest limits. A dense wall of yew forms both a barrier against the west winds and a portico around the main basin at the tip of the promontory, affording delightful glimpses of the garden with the house behind it. Graceful motifs have been incorporated in the pebble paving of the paths and also the date of rebuilding : 1956.

For the visitor the country around Florence is at its most tempting in the spring, the time of year that Petrarch praised :

> *Zephyr returns, bringing the*
> *pleasant season*
> *Of flowers and herbs and all*
> *its sweet array.*

The fields are carpeted with purple anemones. The view is filled with green upon green : the tender, young shade of the growing corn; the infinitely sombre tones of the cypresses, 'dark and pointed', said Boylesve, 'like swords in funeral parades'. I see them rather as brush-strokes when a bend in the road suddenly reveals one outlined against the sky, perhaps by itself or with two or three others a little way off. These trees are often used to mark the entrance or the boundaries of a *podere*, one of the small farms leased to Tuscan peasants under the

métayage system. The house with its tiled roof can be seen half-way up the hill; there, under the trees, stands the tall terracotta oil jar, and the vines are trained in stiff rows running up to the summit. This land with its often

VILLA DELLA PETRAIA: FOUNTAIN BY GIAMBOLOGNA

difficult and stony soil has much in common with Greece, and the scenery is just the same as when the *quattrocento* artists knew and painted it.

If you went the round of the galleries before actually setting eyes

VILLA GAMBERAIA: THE GARDEN

VILLA GAMBERAIA

upon the countryside you will be constantly reminded by this view or that scene of the backgrounds in some of the pictures you looked at and liked not long since. Here, for instance, are the ruffled hilltops, where wayward paths twist and turn, before which passes the Duchess of Urbino's

CERTOSA DEL GALLUZZO: THE CLOISTER

GALLUZZO

chariot with its two unicorns in Piero della Francesca's *Triumph*. That is the peaceful valley bordered by woods and fields seen in the background of Botticelli's *Man with a Medal*. There, again, are the massive cypresses and near-by pine trees that add a note of mystery to Leonardo da Vinci's *Annunciation ;* these others, slender and tapering, can be found in Fra Angelico's *Descent from the Cross*, while those, like the stylized creations of a Japanese artist, are seen in the airy landscape of Iacopo del Sellaio's *St Jerome in the Wilderness*.

Among the villages on the left bank there is one on the Strada Chiantigiana which goes by the name of Grassina. Unobtrusive and hard-working, like all its neighbours, it comes into prominence on one day in the year : Good Friday. It lies to the south-east of Florence, on the way to Siena, in the

SANTA MARIA IMPRUNE

valley of the Ema. Amid this melancholy landscape an imposing ceremony takes place on that day, beginning at the church and ending at a hill close by which represents Calvary complete with the three crosses looking like bare black gibbets against the red-stained sky of the fading day. There, when night has fallen, comes a procession consisting of Roman lictors and a maniple of horsemen, men bearing the emblems of Palm Sunday, then the Sanhedrin, Judas, Peter — all silent actors in the sacred drama. At length, after Longinus, the three Marys with their vases of perfumes and then the Apostles, there follow the image of the dead Redeemer and, as in similar processions in Spain, the figure of the Madonna of the Sorrows, *Maria Santissima Addolorata*. Afterwards the cavalcade of nearly 500 people re-forms by the light

THE FLOWERS OF L'IMPRUNETA

of torches and continues its interminable progress through the streets of
the little town, passing between the close-packed ranks of spectators,
local inhabitants and sightseers together.

There is something very impressive about this 300-year-old tradition
which has been kept up so religiously. But the stream of visitors it draws
from the country roundabout is too much inclined to make this day of
mourning into a day of carnival. And, after all, the important fairs of the
middle ages grew up as a result of the great liturgical festivals. Thus,
at L'Impruneta, a short distance from Grassina, an extremely well-known
fair used to be held each year on the feast of St Luke (18 October). The
basilica of Santa Maria, dating from the eleventh century and rebuilt in
the fifteenth, contains two charming works by Luca della Robbia.

L'Impruneta is quite far out from Florence, but to get back to the
city it is only a matter of going down to Le Tavarnuzze again. On the
way you will certainly not want to miss the Certosa del Galluzzo, which is
interesting from every point of view. First, for its situation on a hill
covered with cheerful orchards and overlooking the confluence of the
Ema and the Greve; next, for its artistic riches; and finally because it is
a typical example of the foundations in the late middle ages which were
endowed by the wealthy and powerful in order to ensure their own eternal
salvation.

Such a patron was Niccolò Acciaiuoli, who belonged to one of
those flourishing banking families with interests everywhere. In politics he
met with much success at the court of Naples and defended the country
against enemies of every type. Honours and titles were showered upon
him, and this aroused the bitter jealousy of his old friend Boccaccio.
Even the Florentines feared this man who had become a very powerful
lord, and in 1341 he invited the priors of the Charterhouses at Muggiano

and Bologna toe stablish a monastery on the large estate that he generously bequeathed to them. Work began on this building straight away but it was by no means finished when the munificent donor died in 1365. The following year Niccolò was buried in the Certosa alongside one of his sons who had died at an early age. These tombs, the work of Florentine craftsmen at the end of the fourteenth century, will be pointed out by the father who shows you round the famous chapel which generations of Florentines have filled to overflowing with treasures, and the spacious cloister designed in the style of Brunelleschi and decorated, like the peristyle of the Spedale degli Innocenti, with medallions by the Della Robbia.

Images of dawn, of high noon and of sunset crowd together in the memory: the glassy pools of Gamberaia, the olive trees in the valley, the massive shape of the Certosa silhouetted against the sky....

MONTE OLIVETO

THE ROOFS OF FLORENCE

PIAZZALE MICHELANGIOLO

CONCLUSION

O happy city, I exclaimed, blessed
With your joyous zephyrs bringing life,
And waters that the Apennines pour down !
                               ... The moon
Clothes in her limpid light your hills
Where the merry vintage reigns; your vales
Hold safe men's homes and olive groves
And waft a thousand flower-scents to the skies.

I read again this evening these lines from Ugo Foscoli's *Sepolcri*
written in praise of the old Guelph city. Now at the end of my journey

219

the incomparable landscape was spread before me once more, but seen from yet another angle : not from Bellosguardo or Fiesole but the top of the Incontro.

This is situated to the east of the city and at over 1,800 feet is the highest point in the environs; you get to it on foot in less than two hours from Bagno a Ripoli. At one time it was very wild and thickly wooded — the Blessed Gerardo da Villamagna, one of the early Franciscan Tertiaries, built his hermitage in this spot. In the eighteenth century St Leonard

GIARDINO DI BOBOLI

PORTA SAN GALLO

of Port Maurice established a monastery here which is still occupied by
the Capuchins. What gives the Incontro its special quality is its silence,
the purity of the air one breathes here, its absolute isolation : for on the
summit of the mountain a grove of cypresses encircles the monastery,
cutting it off completely from the common world of the vine-growers
and gardeners inhabiting the slopes. The view stretches for miles all

LOOKING ACROSS THE PONTE VECCHIO

round this peak; to the west, the blurred lines of the Duomo can be distinguished through the perpetual mist that rises from the Arno.

There are cities which one feels it is impossible to leave. Many writers have had such feelings about Toledo, Marrakesh, Istanbul, Venice, Bruges. Florence exerts an equally strong pull on those who love it, clinging like ivy to their very souls. And who would wish to free themselves from that embrace?

As is often the case with those who love, one ceases to resist or reflect: what do mere reasons matter? What is the point of analysing this exaltation, this almost physical sensation of lightness, of completeness ? Might not this perfect joy be spoilt, the dream vanish ?

Yet it is not so. The more you define your impressions the more conscious you are of the depth and sincerity of your happiness. It takes more than just the beauty of this city to create this sense of well-being. The loveliness reflected in the waters of its river, roaming in the green of its parks, caught in the cornices of its roofs, has a more than material element. The indefinable quality that makes its splendour something unearthly stems as much from the verses of Politian and the bronzes of Donatello as from the experiments of Galileo. The impassioned *terza rima* of Dante is as much part of the city as the *morbidezza* of Botticelli. Florence has seen everything : the spectacular feasts and 'triumphs' of Lorenzo's era and the ravages of the plague ; siege, famine, pomp and the ostentatious extravagance of parvenus ; great councils and royal entrances ; the rod of the tyrant and the open flood-gates of anarchy. But it has never ceased to construct, to produce artists, poets, sculptors, ceramists, engineers, musicians — and saints, many saints ! Of them all Florence might be permitted to say, with Cornelia : 'These are my only jewels !'

FLORENTINE WINDOW

PIAZZA SAN GIOVANNI: PILLAR OF ST ZENOBIUS

INDEX

Names of buildings, piazzas, streets etc. in and outside FLORENCE are printed in bold type.

Names of persons are *italicized*.

Numerals in bold type refer to illustrations.

227

Pliny, 90.
Poggi (Giuseppe) [2nd half of 19th cent.], 194.
Poggio a Caiano (Villa), 204.
Poggio Imperiale, 193.
Poitiers, 45.
Politian, Angelo Poliziano, 29, 108, 109, 136, 164, 223.
Ponte Vecchio, 19, 24, 33, 114, 173, **182,** 183, **222.**
Pontormo, Iacopo Carrucci [1494-1557], 112, 145, 184.
Por Santa Maria (Via), 33, 69, 173, 174.
Porretta (Passo della), 21.
Porsenna, 89.
Portugal (Cardinal James of), 194, 203.
Post Office (Central), 126.
Prato, 28, 29, 193.
Prato (Porta al), 203.
Pratolini, 87.
Proconsolo (Via), 174.
Procopius, 23.
Pucci (family), 163.
Puccio Capanna [14th cent.], 173.

Rabelais (François), 169.
Raphael, Raffaello Sanzio [1483-1520], 109, 116, **116, 118, 119, 120, 121.**
Reni (Guido) [1575-1642], 174.
Reparata, Santa, 51, 58.
Repubblica (Piazza), 22, 66, 174.
Ricasoli (Bettino), 32.
Riccardi (Palazzo), see **Medici-Riccardi.**
Riccardiana (Biblioteca), 161.
Rifredi, 20.
Ripoli (Badia a), 23.
Robbia (Della), **27,** 174. See *Andrea, Giovanni* and *Luca.*
Robert, king of Naples, 27.
Rodolico (Niccolò), 28.
Rolland (Romain), 156.
Roma (Via), 22.
Romana (Porta), 33, 190.
Romanelli (Romano) [20th cent.], 174.
Rome, the *Romans*, 21, 29, 30, 32, 33, 44, 47, 90, 93, 97, 104, 114, 115, 168, 169.
Rossellino, Bernardo Gamberelli [1409-1464], 164, 194.
Rosso (Gianbattista) [1494-1541], 143.
Rovezzano, 19, 205.
Rubens (Peter Paul) [1577-1640], 72.
Rucellai (family), 163.
Rucellai (Palazzo), 168.

Salmi (Mario), 71.
Salvatore, San (church), 194, **198.**
Salvi, San (abbey), **126-127,** 129.

Sansovino, Andrea Contucci [1460-1529], 93.
Sassetti (chapel), 173.
Savonarola (Girolamo), 29, 59, 69, 109, 121, 149.
Savoy (House of), 203.
Saxony (porcelain of), 21.
Schneider (René), 153.
Serragli (Via), 184.
Sesto Fiorentino, 20, 203.
Settignano, 19, 188, 204, 205.
Sèvres (porcelain of), 21.
Shakespeare (William), 76.
Siena, 15, 30, 69, 136, 169, 214.
Sieve (river), 17.
Signorelli (Luca) [1441-1523], 112, 166, 186.
Signoria (Piazza), 36, **48,** 49, 67, 69.
Sixtus IV, pope, 29.
Sloane, (Sir John), 133.
Soderini (Piero), 29.
Sodoma, Giovanni Antonio Bazzi [1477 ?-1549], 125.
Spirito, Santo (church), 128, 184, **192.**
Stendhal, 133.
Stibbert (Frederick), 204.
Stilicho, 23.
Strozzi (chapel), 165.
Strozzi (Palazzo), 39, 169, **172,** 189.
Strozzi (Piazza), 173.
Strozzi (Roberto), 93.
Strozzi (Via), 22.
Suarès (André), 76, 150.
Sulla, 21, 47.

Tacca (Pietro) [1577-1640], 69, **74, 137.**
Taine (Hippolyte), 58, 160, 174.
Talenti (Francesco) [14th cent.], 63.
Tarchiani (Nello), 109.
Tarquinia, 89.
Tavarnuzze (Le), 216.
Theodolinda, queen of the Lombards, 51.
Thomas (St), 65, 164, 166.
Thomas Aquinas (St), 168, **170-171.**
Tino da Camaino, 128.
Tintoretto, Iacopo Robusti [1518-1594], 121.
Titian, Tiziano Vecellio [1477-1576], 113, **116,** 120, 122, 125, **129.**
Titus, 90.
Tivoli, 204.
Toledo (Eleanor of), 73. 166. 188.
Tornabuoni (family), 164, **168.**
Tornabuoni (Via), 169, 173.
Totila, 23.
Tribolo, 203, 204.
Trinità, Santa (church), **22,** 25, 103, 168, 173, **175, 176-177,** 194.
Trinità, Santa (Ponte), 183, 185.

Turks (the), 151.
Tyrrhenian (Sea), 16.

Uffizi (gallery), 21, 22, 75, 86, 87, 88,
94-113, 114-115, 116, 117, 118, 153,
165, 182.
Ugo, margrave of Tuscany, 83, 84.
Umbria, 114, 120.
Urbino (Dukes of), 90, 104, 214. See
also Lorenzo the Magnificent.

Vacchereccia (Via), 69.
Vallombrosa, 24.
Valois (Charles, Comte de), 26.
Van Orley (Bernard) [1492 ?-1542], 93.
Vasari (Giorgio) [1511-1574], 68, 69,
72, 73, 75, 94, 112, 134, 160, 165.
Vaudoyer (Jean-Louis), 69, 183.
Venice, 28, 29, 114.
Verdi (Via Giuseppe), 139.
Veronese, Paolo Caliari [1528-1588], 164.

Verrocchio, Andrea Cioni [1435-1488],
34, **65**, 68, 72, 82, **83**, 154, 183.
Versailles (château), 115, 189.
Vespucci (Amerigo), 29.
Vespucci, Amerigo (Lungarno), 201.
Victor Emmanuel II, king of Italy, 32,
189, 201, 204.
Vienna (Congress of), 32.
Vigna Nuova (Via), 168.
Villani (Giovanni), 23, 43, 69.
Vincigliata, 45.
Visconti (family), 28.
Vitruvius, 139.
Volterra, 28, 29, 89.
Volterra (da), see Daniele.
Volterrano, Baldassare Franceschini
[1611-1689], 204.

Welliver (Warman), 204

Zenobius (St), **224**.
Zuccari (Taddeo) [1529-1566], 58.

ACKNOWLEDGMENTS

Photographs for this book were taken by:

ÉDITIONS ARTHAUD

Photographer M. Bernard AURY, Paris
Page 55.

Photographer M. BERTAULT, Paris
Pages 53 (bottom left), 162.

Photographer M. FAGE, Bièvres
Pages 15, 16-17, 19, 37, 39, 48, 49, 50-51, 67, 70, 74 top, 76 top
and bottom, 77, 78-79, 81, 130, 131, 166-167, 178, 181, 182, 186-
187, 200, 201, 205, 206-207, 208, 211, 212-213, 214-215, 216, 219,
222, 223.

Photographer M. TRINCANO, Lyon
Pages 25, 27, 30-31 top and bottom, 34, 36 top and bottom, 40,
41, 42, 43, 45, 46, 47, 57, 62, 64, 74 bottom, 85, 86, 132, 135, 137,
152, 171, 172, 179, 180, 192, 195, 196-197, 198, 209, 210, 217,
218, 221, 224.

Fratelli ALINARI, Florence
Pages 18, 20, 21 top and bottom, 22 top and bottom, 23, 38, 52,
53 top and bottom (right), 56 top and bottom, 58 right and left,
59, 61, 65 top and bottom, 71, 80, 82, 83, 84, 87, 89, 90, 91, 92,
95, 96, 98, 99, 100-101, 102, 105, 106, 107, 108 top and bottom,
110-111, 113, 114-115, 116, 118, 119, 120, 121, 122, 124-125, 126-
127 top and bottom, 128, 133, 134, 136, 138, 139 top and bottom,
140-141, 142, 143, 144, 146, 147, 148-149, 150-151, 155, 156-157,
158, 159, 160 top and bottom, 161, 165 bottom, 169, 170, 175,
176-177, 188, 189, 190, 191.

ANDERSON, Rome
Pages 117, 129, 145, 165 top, 168.

Signor BROGI, Florence
Pages 60, 97.

Gabinetto Fotografico della
SOPRINTENDENZA ALLE ANTICHITA D'ETRURIA, Florence
Page 88.

M. E.-R. LABANDE, Poitiers
Pages 14, 44, 185, 199, 202, 220.

David LEES, Florence
Page 12.

Signor MANNELLI, Florence
Page 123.